Marx, Engels, and the Workers of the World

Marx, Engels, and the Workers of the World

by Edward Rice

Four Winds Press   New York

LIBRARY OF CONGRESS CATALOGING IN PUBLICATION DATA

Rice, Edward E.
  Marx, Engels, and the workers of the world.

  Includes index.
  SUMMARY: Biographies of the theoreticians whose interpretations of
socialism and communism have been adopted by much of the world's
population.
    1. Marx, Karl, 1818–1883—Juvenile literature. 2. Engels, Frie-
drich, 1820–1895—Juvenile literature. 3. Communists—Biography
—Juvenile literature. 4. Communism—Juvenile literature.
[1. Marx, Karl, 1818–1883. 2. Engels, Friedrich, 1820–1895. 3.
Communists. 4. Communism]
I. Title.
HX39.5.R48   335.4′092′4 [B]   76–56183
ISBN 0-590-07407-5

PUBLISHED BY FOUR WINDS PRESS
A DIVISION OF SCHOLASTIC MAGAZINES, INC., NEW YORK, N.Y.
COPYRIGHT © 1977 BY EDWARD RICE
ALL RIGHTS RESERVED
PRINTED IN THE UNITED STATES OF AMERICA
LIBRARY OF CONGRESS CATALOG CARD NUMBER: 76–56183
1 2 3 4 5   81 80 79 78 77

Contents

Into the bay of communism,
>>>>>>>still fogged
>>>>>>>>>>>>>with blinding mystery,
we thought
>>>>the waves of chance alone
>>>>>>>>>>could bring us
>>>>>>>>>>>>>from our hell.
Marx
>>>>disclosed
>>>>>>>>the deepest
>>>>>>>>>>>laws of history,
put
>>the proletariat
>>>>>>at the helm.
No,
>>>>Marx's books
>>>>>>>>>aren't merely print and paper,
not dust-dry manuscripts
>>>>>>>>>>with dull statistic figures.
His books
>>>>>>brought order
>>>>>>>>>>to the straggling ranks of labor
and led them forward,
>>>>>>full of faith and vigour.

VLADIMIR MAYAKOVSKY

Mayakovsky (born 1893) was a Russian intellectual who welcomed the Revolution of 1917. Though he was an enthusiastic supporter of the new Russia in his poetry, plays, and painting, he was eventually denounced by orthodox Marxist critics for not being close enough to the proletariat. By 1929 and 1930 his new works were totally ignored by all the important writers and critics. He shot himself without explanation in April, 1930. Five years after Mayakovsky was safely dead, Stalin remarked that he considered him "the most talented Soviet poet." Mayakovsky is now a Soviet cultural hero, "the drummer of the Revolution."

If a young man is not a Communist,
there is something wrong with his heart.

If an old man is a Communist,
there is something wrong with his head.

—1930s radical folk wisdom

Introduction

There is probably no single individual since Jesus Christ and the Islamic Prophet Muhammad who has had such a great effect upon the world as Karl Marx, the impoverished, raspish, brilliant, and scholarly theoretician who gave the world his special interpretation of socialist and communist doctrines. Today, after some sixty years of revolutions and coups inspired by Marx's teachings, more than a third of the world's population lives under communist governments, the two great examples being Russia and China. All of central Europe and the Balkans are communist, as well as most of southeast Asia; a communist nation, Cuba, lies within ninety miles of the United States. And many democratic nations have substantial and powerful communist parties. The rest of the world either accepts ideas Marx promulgated, though in limited forms, or at least has been forced to respond to them through social changes of a more democratic nature. And there are a number of nations, especially in Latin America and south Africa, who use the threat of communism, supposed or real, to excuse their own forms of totalitarianism.

Although many of the planks in Marx's various platforms, such as trade unionism, the abolition of child labor, equal rights for women, free education for all, old-age pensions, and social security, were advocated by many other early social thinkers, Marx made them a specific part of his program for revolution. As the present century nears an end, virtually all capitalist countries accept these ideas as a matter of course, some following Marx's teachings by nationalizing banks, utilities, railways, and the means of communication. A few have even instituted heavy taxation of large incomes and of inheritances, as Marx taught.

Marx was in no sense the founder of communism; he said as much on a number of occasions. He did, however, add his own genius to communist and socialist concepts developed by others, putting them into what he and his followers called a scientific framework. Man had long sought for the perfect state, the state in which everyone would have enough material goods to ensure a happy life, and where oppression was absent. The classical Greek philosopher Plato, in his *Republic,* described a state which would be governed by philosophers aided by warriors. Plato put the emphasis on a perfectly functioning state as the central necessity, not on the people, though they would benefit from the harmonious structure under which they lived. Marx was eventually to seek a social structure in which the state would wither away. In the beginning he denounced such a concept as anarchism, but later came to seek it as the logical conclusion of a well-functioning system.

In the *Republic* there was to be no private property; not even the guardians of the state could own anything, and their homes might be entered by any citizen. The rulers were not to receive anything but food for their services. The family was to be abolished; children would be born of sexual union licensed by the state; the more distinguished guardians would enjoy the privilege of more frequent union with the more beautiful women. Plato's better world, it might be seen, like other schemes to follow, was constructed on a sexist basis. Children would be raised by the state. Imperfect individuals were to be destroyed, a principle to be extended even to intellectual fields. The arts were put into a special category: those works (like Hesiod's and Homer's) which suggested that the gods were imperfect, or contained gloomy or disrespectful themes, would be destroyed; at the same time works considered aesthetically perfect were to be considered suspect and dangerous.

Plato's ideas survived the centuries and helped fertilize the rebellions of the Middle Ages, of which there were many, protesting both the frightful living conditions and the imposition of religous doctrines the people could not accept. Movements considered heretical by the orthodox Christians, like the Anabaptists, who rejected infant baptism, advocated alike the destruction of the ruling classes and the sharing of all property, which in those ages included not only land and buildings but women and children. The Apostolic Brethren of thirteenth-century Italy preached that "in love everything must be held in common—property and wives." A century later the Taborites of central Europe taught "there is no Mine or Thine, everybody uses everything equally; all must hold everything in common, and nobody must have anything separately, and he who does is a sinner. . . . Everything, including wives, must be held in common." Such movements were more than communistic, they were anarchistic, and all semblance of rule was to be destroyed: "All those who have been elevated and given power must be bent like the twigs of trees and cut down, burned in the stove like straw, leaving not a root nor a shoot, they must be ground like sheaves, the blood must be drained from them, they must be killed by scorpions, snakes and wild animals, they must be put to death."

The historian I. von Döllinger sums up the movements in general by saying:

> Every heretical movement that appeared in the Middle Ages possessed, openly or secretly, a revolutionary character; in other words, if it had come to power it would have had to destroy the existing social order and produce a political and social revolution. These Gnostic sects, the Catharists and Albigensians, whose activities evoked severe and implacable legislation against heresy and were bloodily opposed, were socialists and communists. They attacked marriage, the family and property.

The authorities, no matter who they were, realized the implications of the revolts. When, in the early sixteenth century, the peasants of Germany and Austria rose up against their feudal overlords, who were often prince-bishops, they expected support from the great Protestant leader Martin Luther. But he too, as much as any Catholic churchman, feared the peasants would replace the entrenched social structure; he denounced the peasants and encouraged their ruthless suppression. For these exploited farm laborers, hardly better than slaves, had boldly announced the end of the exploitative world. One of the peasant leaders (usually called the Zwickau prophets) stated their objectives as follows:

> Any man can take wives when the flesh demands it and his passions rise, and live with them in bodily intimacy exactly as he pleases. Everything is to be held in common, since God sent all people into the world equal. . . . All authorities, terrestrial and spiritual, must be dismissed at once and for all, or be put to the sword, for they live untrammeled, they drink the blood and sweat of their poor subjects, they guzzle and drink night and day. . . . We must fall upon the bloodsuckers, seize their houses, loot their property and raze their castles to the ground.

But while this frenzied search for relief from oppression was being expressed by the German peasants, a calmer view of a better world had already appeared. This was in the great work called *Utopia,* by Sir Thomas More, who was to be sainted by the Catholic Church for his refusal to put expediency over conscience in a quarrel with his king, England's Henry VIII, who had him beheaded. In *Utopia,* published in 1516, More continued with many of Plato's concerns, the chief being an ideal state founded upon communist principles. More was not an idle dreamer. He saw that the world was changing rapidly —it was the age of the great explorations of other continents and of the rise of the merchant class—and he believed that plans had to be outlined for the benefit of the world. In his scathing critique of English society, he often spoke in forceful images:

> Your sheep that are wont to be so meek and tame and such small eaters, now, as I hear say, have become such great devourers and so wild that they eat up and swallow down the very men themselves.

But he was not merely pointing out that animals were being treated better than the peasants who kept them. This pastoral image has another meaning, for at this time the king's favorites were seizing the English monasteries which had been so important in developing the wool industry and destroying the very means of production which had helped make them and the country wealthy. The sheep were a symbol of the uncontrolled greed of men freed from the rules of society. More's solution to such problems was an ideal state, tightly structured so that sheep would not devour men in any sense, where each person would fit into a regulated, happy, well-fed life.

Utopia advocated common ownership of property, with bureaucratic rule and compulsory labor; More included slavery both as a valuable economic asset and as a punishment to ensure the stability of society. His Utopian world also restricted free movement outside one's own city and prescribed standardized clothing and housing; however, certain people would be free to change jobs.

Utopia—which soon lent its name to the concept of the ideal, often impractical state—was followed by a flood of similar works, communist in thought. *The City of the Sun,* published in 1602 by the Italian monk Tommaso Campanella, contained many of More's ideas, but the author stressed the importance of people in groups, and government control of sexual relations and the family. In 1652 *The Law of Freedom in a Platform* by the Englishman Gerrard Winstanley duplicated much of More. The utopian theme became the subject of a series of romantic novels, often set in strange, faraway backgrounds. Among these were Verras's *The History of the Savarambi,* Fontenelle's *The Republic of Philosophers* and de la Bretonne's *The Southern Discovery.* Philosophical and didactic works with a utopian theme also abounded. In all of these works, including *Utopia,* a latent hostility to religion was manifest. Meslier's *Testament* sees religion as the cause of the world's misfortunes and not only a superstition but an absurdity. He attacks Christ in long tirades since "he was always poor" and "he wasn't resourceful enough." Other works, such as the very influential *Law of Nature* by Morelly (published 1755), state themes later to be found in Marx and his followers: "no private property except objects in daily use" and each person to be kept employed on behalf of society in order to "contribute for his part to the general wealth according to his powers, his talents and his age."

The urge for the perfect society is basic to the human soul and reappears in virtually every era. Immediately after the end of World War II, the behaviorist psychologist B. F. Skinner wrote a novel which put the utopian theme into a modern frame (though like other utopian novelists he places the locale in a mythical country). *Walden Two,* named after Henry Thoreau's book, *Walden,* which describes the nineteenth-century philosopher's year in simple isolation at Walden Pond in Massachusetts, is the same theme applied to a well-financed community of a thousand people, whose utopia is motivated not by economics or politics but psychological concepts. Skinner believes that problems of the modern world will not be solved with more or better machines nor with a return to a simpler less materialistic life, but with a conditioned change in the human personality. His techniques of behavioral engineering are the guiding theme.

Life in *Walden Two* is communal. In order to attain the good life for all, the community is to be conditioned by strictly controlled psychological techniques, beginning with childhood. The community is austere, disciplined, almost puritanical; it is self-supporting, with its own farms, dairy, flocks of sheep, mills, medical staff, theater groups, symphony orchestra (but no rock), and community kitchens. The managers are appointed, and work and property of all members are shared through a system of labor credits. The more odious tasks (like cleaning the barns) earn better "pay." Monogamous marriages are preferred to free liaisons. Children are raised by the community. Skinner suggests that couples have their children early—in their late teens and early twenties, the healthiest time for reproduction—after which they will be able to engage in pursuits other than child rearing. Unlike the common sharing of women proposed by so many of the earlier utopias, *Walden Two* says that too much sexual play is "a sign, not of potency, but of malaise or instability."

In this present age, in which communes have proliferated, Skinner believes that the collapse of many of them has come because the members want an immediate gratification of ideals and goals, put too much emphasis on an agrarian way of life, and have lacked capital. Whether or not *Walden Two* offers a practical blueprint for utopian communities, the *idea* has been a success, for the book has sold some million copies since its publication in 1946. Yet there has been much antagonism to it; its critics charge the work offers a barely disguised totalitarianism, with the fictional members being brainwashed into utopianism.

The vision of a better world eventually had to come down to earth, and the new democratic governments of the United States and France founded near the end of the eighteenth century were based on some of these principles. But such egalitarian examples of liberty and brotherhood were not enough for many communists, for there were still too many members of the exploiting classes. A number of attempts were made to establish truly communist societies. Communism in practice, not theory, was, to give a single example, the aim of a secret French society called the Union of the Equals, founded, or at least uncovered, in 1786. The members of the union had preached the abolition of private property and the centralization of the entire economy. The basic theme was that "the Fatherland takes possession of a man from the day of his birth and does not let go of him until his very death." Life was to be lived in common, with communal refectories; censorship was to be introduced, freedom of movement was forbidden and everyone had to work for the state. The uncooperative, the dissolute, and the lazy were to be condemned to forced labor on isolated islands.

There were valid and very pressing reasons for these yearnings for the perfect state, in which justice would prevail over oppression. Living conditions for all but those on top of the social pyramid were abysmal. The life span was short, housing was primitive, food inadequate, and famines were common, and everyone was subject to the whim of those above. "In a word," wrote Marx in *The Communist Manifesto,* "oppressor and oppressed stood in constant opposition to one another [and] carried on an uninterrupted, now hidden, now open fight, a fight that each time ended, either on a revolutionary re-constitution of society at large, or in the common ruin of the contending classes." Though historians might have divided the world into freeman and slave, patrician and plebeian, lord and serf, guild master and journeyman, or into various classes of social ranks —knights, plebeians, slaves, feudal lords, vassals, guild-masters, journeymen, apprentices and serfs, and so on—the world, Marx was to point out, had merely simplified itself into "two great hostile camps" as class antagonisms had clarified over the centuries. The vast upheavals of the Middle Ages, in which society had been shattered by plagues, the Crusades, peasant rebellion, and religious reformation, helped produce the burghers—the new class of businessmen—of the earliest towns, whose descendants were to be known as the bourgeoisie. These, Friedrich Engels, Marx's collaborator, defined as the "class of modern Capitalists, owners of the means of social production and employers of wage labour." The bourgeoisie were one of Marx's two hostile camps. The other was the new class of the proletariat, whom Engels defined as "the class of modern wage-labourers, who, having no means of production of their own, are reduced to selling their labour power in order to live." Such were the opposing forces. There was, however, a third major force, the state, exemplified in some cases by such feudal relics as emperors, kings, and nobles, or in the modern world by duly elected democratic governments. In any case, Marx and Engels saw the state, in whatever form, as an enemy to be replaced first by the bourgeoisie who would in turn be replaced by the proletariat.

The rise of the bourgeoisie had come slowly, with the discovery of the Americas, the opening up of East-Indian and Chinese markets, and the finding of vast new sources of raw material in other parts of the world, which could be had for little more than a show of military force and token payments. What precipitated the crisis between the bourgeoisie and its source of labor was the Industrial Revolution of the eighteenth century. James Watt's steam engine, invented in 1765, coupled with some simple inventions in related fields, led to the development of industry on a large scale. Commercial production of the steam engine in quantity was made possible by the invention of a boring device by the ironmaster John Wilkinson, which could ream out cannon barrels and the cylinders of the Watt engine with equal facility. Thus improvements in the factory led to improved weaponry and to a radicalizing of warfare as well as industry. The Watt invention was eminently adaptable. One of

Watt's first two machines built with Wilkinson's boring methods was put to work forcing air into Wilkinson's pig-iron blast furnaces. This was a crucial step, for it meant that expensive charcoal would now be replaced with cheap coke. The steam engine pumped fresh air into the newly opened mines, and flood water out, and helped raise the coal; thus workers could reach lodes unattainable before. It provided power for factories, especially the great cotton mills of the English Midlands. Improved models were to power the steam locomotive, the steam tug and the steamboat, not only making travel easier for the individual but enabling industry to loot the colonial world of raw materials, ship them to England, and return them in finished form to be sold at prices lower than the indigenous handcrafted pieces. "The plains of India are white with the bleached bones of the Indian weavers," said a report in the British Parliament, in discussing the plight of one of the most tragic victims, for the English spinning jennies were producing cloth for India out of Indian cotton cheaper than could be woven on the subcontinent. Numerous other developments accompanied the Industrial Revolution. Quite early the first steel bridges were constructed, thus speeding traffic; a system of inland canals was dug to move raw materials and finished produce.

The social structure was now being measured in terms of productivity. The verdant green of the English poets was soon covered with a layer of soot; the slag heap replaced the forest. The country village lay empty as the industrial slum began to grow. The human cost of the new wealth passed belief. Whole areas of the countryside were emptied of their men, women, and children to provide labor for the mines, mills, and factories. Slums, shortened lives, illness, broken families, drunkenness, drug addiction, prostitution followed on a large scale. Numerous protests took place, not only in England, the most advanced industrial nation, but in France, Germany, and Central Europe. In England, workers in the late eighteenth and early nineteenth century, calling themselves Luddites after one of their leaders, broke up the new machines introduced into the factories. The worst protests came during the period 1811-16 when Luddites smashed the new knitting machines in protest against the resulting unemployment and reduced pay. Brutal reprisal followed; in 1819 a mass meeting of workers in Manchester brought a savage repression by the militia against people looking for redress from reactionary legislation; the result was known as the Peterloo Massacre, a bitter play on Waterloo. The poet Shelley wrote in the victims' memory, "Rise, like lions after slumber, In unvanquishable number, Shake your chains to earth like dew . . . "

In 1834, when six farm hands, soon known as the Tolpuddle Martyrs, tried to organize, they were given seven-year sentences in Australia; the public protest resulted in their eventual release. The Chartist movement of the 1830s, named after the Magna Charta of 1215, which attempted to prevent royal abuse by the king and maintain the feudal privileges of the barons and the bishops, tried to gain basic rights for the working people. The Chartists led many protest movements on behalf of the workers; at one point they gained 3,500,000 signatures on petitions. Skillful opposition by government and industrialists and bad Chartist leadership eventually brought the movement to an end. On the continent protests took place constantly. In 1831 and again in 1834 the weavers of Lyons erupted in bitter rebellion, only to be put down. One of their revolutionary songs goes—

> When our reign comes
> Yours shall end

Then we'll weave the old world's shroud.

And when the weavers of Silesia, a German state, revolted in 1844, the poet Heinrich Heine wrote:

Old Germany, we are weaving a shroud for you
And weaving it with a triple curse
We are weaving, weaving.

The conditions under which the workers of the Industrial Revolution existed are hard to imagine today. England, as the pioneer in the factory system, was the leading offender. Many people were concerned, and numerous commissions and investigative bodies, most official but sometimes of private citizens, sought to lay bare the horror of the workers' lives and bring about reforms. Blue books and white papers told of children sleeping next to their machines, too tired to go home, after work days of fourteen and eighteen hours—if they had a home. Instances were recorded of many occasions of children working thirty hours at a stretch in fearful dust, dirt and heat, in factories, mills, and mines. Investigations of railway accidents revealed that the engineers had been forced to drive as many as fifty hours, and in one case, eighty hours, without sleep. But the worst abuses were in the employment of children and women, for they had little chance of protest. Some of the children were as young as seven. A case was noted of a working father who carried his son to the factory on his back and who had to feed the boy at the wallpaper printing machine, for the machine could not stop—rather the owner would not let it stop—during a sixteen-hour day. The lot of women was just as cruel. Not only did they stand at the bottom of the work hierarchy, not being allowed to rise to supervisory positions, but they were subject to sexual abuse, from foremen and owners' sons and from co-workers as well. Women in the mines did the same jobs as men but for less pay. Numerous cases are recorded of women being forced to extend a sixteen-hour day to twenty-four. Conditions were so bad, in the eyes of Parliament, that in 1833 steps were taken to reduce the working hours of children of thirteen or younger to eighteen per day. (On the continent it was twelve.) In 1844 the House of Commons set the children's workday at twelve hours in most factories and eight in a few. But there were many objections on the part of industrialists. The silk manufacturers, for example, objected that a shorter day would rob the children of their "liberty" to enjoy adequate working time; these were children, a government inspector noted, who were often so small—employed because of their "lightness of touch" in handling delicate fabrics—that they had to be lifted to their work stools at the machines. Women over eighteen, no longer considered as children, benefited from the same legislation during this period, but, needless to say, there were many ways of getting around the laws.

But men led no better lives. The statement about to be quoted can find its parallel in numerous reports. This is by a Dr. J. T. Arledge:

> The potters as a class, both men and women, represent a degenerated population, both physically and morally. They are, as a rule, stunted in growth, ill-shaped, and frequently ill-formed in the chest; they become prematurely old, and are certainly short-lived. They are phlegmatic and bloodless, and exhibit their debility of constitution by obstinate attacks of dyspepsia, and disorders of the liver and kidneys, and by rheumatism. But of all diseases they are especially prone to chest-disease, to pneumonia, phthisis, and asthma. One form would appear peculiar to them, and is known as potter's asthma, or potter's consumption. Scrofula attacking the glands, or bones, or other parts of

the body, is a disease of two-thirds or more of the potters. . . .

To add to the misery, the food the working classes got was of the worst types. In an investigation of the baking industry, which revealed the usual degradation—men forced to sleep in their place of employment so as to be ready when needed, frightful heat, unpaid labor, and so on—it was shown that the Englishman's daily bread was something other than what he expected. The report, Marx was to comment, "roused not the heart of the public but its stomach." For in the bread was commonly found "a certain quantity of human perspiration mixed with the discharge of abscess, cobwebs, dead black-beetles, and putrid German yeast, without counting alum, sand, and other agreeable mineral ingredients." A French chemist named Chevallier, meanwhile, had enumerated the problems of adulteration in his own country: such as six kinds of adulteration of sugar, nine of olive oil, ten of butter, twelve of salt, nineteen of milk, twenty of bread, twenty-four of meal, twenty-eight of chocolate, thirty of wine, thirty-two of coffee, and so on.

Marx depended heavily upon these government and private investigations, not only to underscore the conditions of the working classes, but to help support his basic theories about capital. In his great work *Das Kapital,* he was to say:

> Capital is dead labour, that vampire-like, only lives by sucking living labour, and lives the more, the more labour it sucks. The time during which the labourer works, is the time during which the capitalist consumes the labour-power he has purchased of him. And the capitalist "is only capital personified."
>
> His soul is the soul of capital. But capital has one single life impulse, the tendency to create value and surplus-value, to make

its constant factor, the means of production, absorb the greatest
possible amount of surplus-labour.

Such is the background of Karl Marx's world, two hostile,
incompatible forces locked in a ruthless struggle, which he
repeatedly emphasized could have but one conclusion, the victory of the workers over the capitalists. It was obviously and
simply a war to the death, as he saw it. George Bernard Shaw,
the Anglo-Irish socialist and playwright, was to make the comment that Marx "wrote about capitalists and workers like a
class-war correspondent." And when Marx's first famous work,
The Communist Manifesto, finally emerged from obscurity,
with its ringing conclusion, "Workers of the world unite, you
have nothing to lose but your chains," it was no wonder that
the proletariat were stirred to the depths of their wretched
souls.

1

The Young Marx

The Birth of a Revolutionary   The year was 1818, the
month May, and the day the fifth. The place was Trier (otherwise Trèves), an ancient city in the Rhineland, the fertile, cul-
tured area of Germany which has known civilization longer
than any other, having been colonized by the Romans. The
child born on this day, Karl Marx, was the son of Heinrich
Marx and Henrietta Pressberg, both Jews from a long rabbinical lineage. The world in which the Marxes lived was repressive
and restrictive, for although conditons were gradually chang-

The house in Trier, where Karl Marx was born, March, 1818.

ing, Jews in Europe and elsewhere faced many of the limiting regulations and laws that had originated in the Dark Ages of the West. The ancestors of the new child had been forced to wander about Europe, finding refuge here and there in homes that they hoped would be permanent but would have to abandon after a generation or so. It was the fate of Jews to migrate from one country to another in search of safety from anti-Semitic laws.

Heinrich Marx, whose own father, Marx ha-Levi (the name is spelled in various ways), and grandfather had been rabbis in the Rhineland, could trace his ancestry back over four centuries. Ironically, these ancestors had fled Germany because of the intense persecution of the Jews. They had found homes in Italy, Poland, and the Ukraine, only to return again to Germany. Henrietta Pressberg (or Pressborck) could trace her ancestry to another famous line of rabbis, the first of whom was known to have lived in Hungary. Her grandfather (or perhaps great-grandfather) had emigrated to the Netherlands in search of freedom, finding a home in the old city of Neimegen.

Heinrich Marx, who was born Hirschel ha-Levi in 1782 in Sauerlaten in the Rhineland, saw during his lifetime improved treatment of Jews in this part of Europe. The year before his birth, the counselor of the Prussian Court at Berlin, Christian Wilhelm Dorn, in a polemical work, *Concerning the Civic Amelioration of the Jews,* attacked the Christian world for the degradation and social stagnation it had imposed on Jews. The American and French revolutions put Jews on the same footing as everyone else, though in France the struggle for equality was hard won. When the French emperor Napoleon invaded his neighboring states, he proclaimed the emancipation of the Jews. But in 1806, when he called a council of the leading rabbis in France, severe restrictions were placed upon French Jews, although the Jewish population in Prussia and the parts of Germany under French occupation had almost complete freedom. By 1812 they attained full freedom, and it was in this atmosphere of developing equality that Hirschel ha-Levi could leave the Jewish community of his birth, change his name to the more Germanic Heinrich Marx, move to the nearby town of Trier, and become a lawyer, a profession hitherto denied Jews.

Trier had become a sleepy little Rhineland town of some 12,000 people ruled by a Roman Catholic archbishop, although it had once been an opulent and successful wine-making center. In 1803 the troops of the French emperor Napoleon entered the Rhineland, incorporating everything up to the left bank of the Rhine into the empire and ousting the ruling archbishop. Like most Rhinelanders, Heinrich Marx welcomed the French. The area, which was the most developed part of Germany, had long been influenced by French ideas, most importantly by the battle cry of the Revolution, "Liberty, Equality, and Brotherhood." French culture was popular, and there had been uprisings among both peasants and the liberal middle class, who were influenced by the freedom they observed in the neighboring country.

Napoleon broke up the big estates of the landed gentry, abolished feudal privileges, encouraged the development of industry, and introduced trial by jury and other legal rights according to the Code Napoleon, then a radical departure from the oppressive feudal laws of the time. The emperor next turned his attention to other parts of Europe, culminating in his disastrous defeats in Russia (1812) and Leipzig (1813), his temporary exile at Elba, his ultimate defeat at Waterloo (1815), and his subsequent banishment to St. Helena.

With this turn of events, Heinrich Marx had come face to face again with the deep-rooted and almost ineradicable fact of anti-Semitism. Since Napoleon was no longer a threat, the German princes and the heads of the other feudal states and cities of Europe met at the Congress of Vienna in 1815 to re-establish themselves and to reapportion their part of Europe. Most of the Rhineland went to Prussia. This most western part of Germany was, in fact, hardly more than a colony of Prussia, with little representation at the court in Berlin; it was the homeland of a people with a different culture, a different accent, and a different economy. It was the only area of Germany with any appreciable industry, and it was completely different in mood and feeling from the great brooding, forested, authoritarian state of Prussia, with its remote aristocracy, professional officer corps, and mystical cult of the military.

Yet, Heinrich Marx, who at times seemed like a rather naive man, had a strange appreciation of this other Germany, and had a great respect for his new king, Friedrich Wilhelm III. Of Heinrich's life little is known. He once stated that he stood by "hard principles," and that "I received nothing from my family, except, I must confess, my mother's love." Years later Karl Marx was to remark of his father that he was "as remarkable for his personal honesty as for his legal talents."

Having rejected his rabbinical background and training, Heinrich Marx took up the ideas of the European Enlightenment, that widespread movement that brought bold, new, rationalist, and practical approaches to all aspects of human thought, from science, the arts, and philosophy to government. His neighbor, Edgar von Westphalen, who was to play a role in young Karl Marx's intellectual development, said of Heinrich that he was a "real eighteenth-century Frenchman, who knew his Voltaire and his Rousseau inside out." Heinrich Marx also read Kant, Locke, Newton, Leibniz, all important influences on European thought of the time. Although his interests were liberal and therefore oriented towards France, Heinrich Marx favored the Prussians over Napoleon, who, although he had given the Jews freedom, had also plundered the Rhineland.

The elder Marx had much to overcome, much of the past to exchange for the new world that he saw arising, and so he did not marry until he was thirty-one, when he took Henrietta Pressberg as his wife in a traditional Jewish ceremony in 1813. The couple settled down in a fashionable house in Trier. Later they moved to an even larger house, where with Marx's income from rents and from his legal practice they were able to live in great comfort and style. Their first child, Moritz-David, was born in 1815 but died soon afterwards. Then came Sophie, in 1816, and after her, Karl, in 1818.

Meanwhile Heinrich Marx was worrying over the problem of race and religion. Though representatives of the Jewish communities had pleaded with the German princes at Vienna in 1815, they were unable to prevent the reimposition of the old anti-Jewish laws and regulations, along with numerous other rules which defined and restricted the roles of Christian peasants, artisans, and workers. Jews were once again barred from all public office, as well as from the practice of law and of pharmacy. Heinrich Marx, with the recommendation of a number of prominent officials of the law courts, petitioned the Minister of the Interior at Berlin for an exception to the anti-Semitic regulations but was denied. So, at the age of thirty-four, in 1816, this progressive young lawyer, who had emancipated himself from the synagogue and had studied and enjoyed the best minds of the Enlightenment, found himself thrown back into the Middle Ages. He was now in an occupational as well as religious and emotional crisis. He decided to become a Christian, not only for practical reasons but also because he sincerely felt an attraction to Christianity. It was a decision being made by other Jews as well. The contemporary historian Hugo Valentin wrote, with only a slight touch of exaggeration, that "during the first eighteen years of the nineteenth century more German Jews were baptized than in the previous eighteen hundred years put together." For some, like the poet Heinrich Heine, it was a means of getting out of the restrictions of the ghetto, for he said frankly, "I was baptized, not converted." And he added in explanation of the plight of the Jews, "Judaism is not a religion but a misfortune."

Though Trier was a predominantly Roman Catholic town, Heinrich Marx turned to Lutheranism because he equated Protestantism with intellectual freedom and because Lutheranism was the religion of Prussia. He was baptized sometime in 1816 or early 1817, and his children in 1824. Henrietta Marx, who delayed her conversion out of respect for her strictly orthodox father, waited until he died in 1825. During this period six more children were born to the Marxes: Hermann in 1819, Henrietta in 1820, Luise in 1821, Emilie in 1822, Karilina in 1824, and Eduard in 1826. Two of the girls and one boy died in early childhood, and of all the Marx children only Karl lived to old age.

It seems to have been a warm and loving family, though little is known of any details, except that the Marxes lived comfortably. Heinrich Marx was said to be a handsome, serious man. One of his granddaughters, on the basis of a daguerreotype, said he was "typically Jewish but beautifully so." Politically, he was a mild liberal, influenced by the French but still loyal to the Prussian government at Berlin, which regarded any kind of liberalism with grave suspicion. There was no doubt about Heinrich Marx's patriotism, though he belonged to a social club which was under suspicion, because its members sang songs at their dinners and entertainments that may have alluded to doctrines not in favor with the government in Berlin. Any slight yearning for "freedom" might bring the police. On one occasion in 1834, Heinrich Marx made a speech praising the king "to whose magnanimity we owe the first steps towards national representation," adding, "Truth should advance to the steps of the throne." The police did not believe that Marx was sincere in his praise of the despotic Prussian ruler but thought he was being sarcastic and expressing his liberal views ironically. He was unfairly denounced as a liberal "from whom no sort of conciliation was to be expected in the present tension between Prussia and the Rhineland"; nevertheless he continued to be a loyal subject of the king.

Henrietta Marx, who grew up in the Netherlands, spoke Dutch as her maternal tongue and her German was imperfect and heavily accented. The children were raised in both languages. She was a superstitious woman and throughout her life was convinced that she would die exactly fifty years to the moment after her marriage, which was at four o'clock on November 20, 1813. Her prophecy was indeed accurate. Since orthodox Jewish women had little education compared to men, she shared none of her husband's intellectual interests. When he was young, Karl called her "angel mother" and "this great, wonderful woman." But later, when he was forced to borrow money from her, and she berated him for wasting the family's fortune at the university, he grew to dislike her. Marx virtually abandoned his mother in her old age, but she was still generous enough to write off the many loans she had made to him. As her son grew and matured into a famous radical, Henrietta Marx understood him less and less, but it was still obvious that she retained her love for him until her death.

Marx's Childhood   Marx's childhood stands as a mystery. Most of the events of his youth, despite the most strenuous research by biographers, are unknown. Anecdotes, incidents, friendships, influences cannot be found to illuminate his growing years and give us a clue to the adult man. At the age of twelve he was sent to the Friedrich-Wilhelm Gymnasium in Trier. The school had been founded by the Jesuits, a leading Roman Catholic order, and though recently secularized, still maintained a strong but unofficial Catholic aura. Thus Marx, the decendant of a long line of rabbis and baptized a Protestant, was to spend five years under Catholic influences. But the religious environment had little effect upon him. What seemed to have been a stronger influence was the school's liberal attitudes. The headmaster, a disciple of the great German philosopher Kant, and some of the teachers were suspected of anti-government sentiments, and so the school was under constant police surveillance.

Marx took not only the usual courses, which at that time included the Greek and Latin classics, history, mathematics, German (his own language), and French, but also religion, which in this case was a liberal form of Catholicism. He became an expert in the ancient tongues, and could translate the classics with care and proficiency, but his French was best described as "industrious." At least, he developed a working knowledge, which he was to employ and develop later during his years in exile in France and Belgium. Mathematics was his weakest subject, and his collaborator, Friedrich Engels, was to complain in later years, when he was trying to decipher Marx's elaborate and often contradictory notes for the second and third volumes of *Das Kapital,* of Marx's hopelessness in handling mathematical equations.

Students of Marx had tried to find some sources of Marx's

later theories in the religious courses he took at the gymnasium, but without success. The long essay on a religious subject that was found among Marx's papers shows only a perfunctory attention to the course assigned by his teacher at the gymnasium. Marx had no religious commitment, no yearnings, and was later to renounce and denounce religion in unsparing terms. He gave a routine answer to the question, speaking of "an inner elevation, comfort in sorrow, calm trust, and a heart susceptible to human love, to everything noble and great, not for the sake of ambition or glory, but only for the sake of Christ."

However, in his German essay, which is entitled "Considerations of a Young Man in Choosing His Career," he showed a considerable amount of idealistic ambition. He wrote that it was not the search for social position that should guide one but a striving for personal fulfillment and working for humanity. Even at this age he thought human beings were formed by extraneous conditions, saying that "to some extent we have already acquired relationships in society before we are in a position to decide them." By founding a career on "ideas that we thoroughly believe in, which affords us the greatest chance of working for humanity," each of us can be "a complete and truly great man." And, "Experience calls him the happiest who has made the most people happy." The essay concludes by saying,

> If we have chosen the position in which we can accomplish the most for humanity, then we can never be crushed by the burdens because these are only sacrifices made for the sake of all. Then it is no poor, restricted, egotistic joy that we savour; on the contrary our happiness belongs to millions, our deeds live on calmly with endless effect; and our ashes will be moistened by the ardent tears of noble men.

This was a rather romantic view of a person who sacrifices himself for humanity, but it was also a broad outline of the program which Marx was to set for himself in the coming years.

Only one close friend of young Marx is known. He was the boy who lived next door, Edgar von Westphalen. His father was a prominent official in the Prussian government, and his sister, Jenny, was the girl whom Marx would some day marry. Young von Westphalen is described as a good-natured and weak man, who followed Marx in his early twenties but then emigrated to Texas, only to lose everything he made. He returned to Europe, recouped his losses, and emigrated a second time to Texas, only to lose everything again. He finally returned to Europe once again, where he remained.

It was Edgar's father, the privy councilor Ludwig von Westphalen, who made the greatest impression upon young Marx and became not only a close friend but something of a second father after Heinrich Marx died. The von Westphalens were a highly placed family. The baron's mother was Scottish, and he grew up speaking English. He also knew French, Spanish, Italian, Latin, and Greek. He was the senior officer in Trier, being the representative of the Prussian court in Berlin. Von Westphalen introduced Marx to the Greek classic poets and Shakespeare, all of whom they read in the original languages together. He also gave Marx the works of the liberal French political theorist, Claude-Henri Saint-Simon. Marx later dedicated his university dissertation to the privy councilor, calling him several times, "My dear fatherly friend." By the time he was eighteen Marx had become deeply attached to Jenny von Westphalen, who was four years his senior.

The baron was a liberal, and he had hoped for a liberalization of the various governments in Germany after Napoleon's fall.

He had been imprisoned by the French for protesting against their heavy taxes upon the Germans, this after welcoming Napoleon as the carrier of revolutionary ideas which would liberate Europe. But he found the French as bad as the Germans, and when the Council of Vienna restored the old order, he accepted a government post and tried to work for an amelioration of conditions among his own people. The baron was in his sixties when he found in young Marx a sympathetic and intelligent companion, more open to liberal ideas than in his own son Edgar. And so the elder von Westphalen and Marx would take daily walks through the woods along the banks of the Moselle river, their conversation ranging from the Greek classics to contemporary politics. Yet there was an invisible wall between the von Westphalens, who were Christian, and the Marxes, who, despite their baptism, were, in the eyes of the world, still Jews. Both the baron and Heinrich Marx realized the impossibility of a marriage between Karl and Jenny, and both, at first subtly, and then directly tried to discourage the romance. But in the autumn of 1836 Karl, then eighteen, and Jenny, twenty-two, became secretly engaged.

Marx at the University   In October, 1835, Marx, still only halfway through his seventeenth year, matriculated at the University of Bonn, not far from Trier. It was a small university, and there was a clear-cut distinction between the students from noble families and the plebeians, as they were called. The courses in which Marx enrolled were, for the most part, continuations of his high school studies on a more advanced level and included Greek and Roman mythology and the history of art. He also began studies in law, which perhaps was the most demanding of his courses.

Marx, aged eighteen, as a student at the University of Bonn, where he spent almost a year at the faculty of law. The portrait is excerpted from the engraving below of the Trier students' club, of which Marx was a member. At Bonn, Marx, as a commoner, got into arguments with students from the nobility, and once was arrested for carrying a gun. This was after he was wounded in a duel with a noble.

One of the features of life at Bonn was the "poetry society." There were a number of them, and they were actually small groups of students dedicated to revolutionary ideas. They were the target of the nobles, and their members engaged in a certain amount of bullying which would often lead to fights. Marx was elected the president of one and began to carry a pistol as a means of warning the nobles that he was not to be harassed. On one occasion he actually fought a duel with a noble and was wounded over the left eye. Another time, while visiting a poetry society at nearby Cologne, he got drunk with some other students, was arrested, and found to have the pistol in his possession. Although carrying a sword or a knife and dueling were signs of manhood, the possession of a pistol was not tolerated, and he had to face charges. After lengthy intercession by his father with the judge, "as one father to another," Marx was released.

It was during this period that the first signs of a lifelong problem began to show themselves: he spent more than he had, and his year at Bonn was marked by extravagant living. His father frequently had to send him supplements to his allowance, and his papers at Bonn indicate that he was often in debt and failed to pay notes.

After finishing the summer term at Bonn, Marx was transferred to the University of Berlin by his father. Berlin was a large city of half a million people, the capital of the Prussian state, and the seat of a power that controlled a large portion of Europe. The university, unlike that at Bonn, had excellent teachers and was demanding of its students. Marx's older contemporary, the philosopher Ludwig Feuerbach, had written to his own father some twelve years previous that "this university is a temple of study and all the others are no more than coffee-houses."

But Marx was to be the exception. Though he found certain intellectual interests that he pursued with the dedication he was capable of bestowing upon subjects that interested him, he also began to drink heavily and to live what was called in the last century a "bohemian life." He attended classes in a desultory manner, and besides leading his active night life, he became interested in writing poetry and highly involuted philosophical essays. His notebooks show assigned readings of Aristotle, Spinoza, Leibniz, Hume, and Kant; his earliest semesters were devoted chiefly to law, which included criminal law and Prussian provincial law, along with formal jurisprudence, but his legal studies soon faded into the background. For a short while he was attracted to anthropology and geography. But then he missed two semesters entirely, being absorbed in his own pursuits and pleasures. During one semester he took but a single course, on the prophet Isaiah, and in another he is recorded as having attended one lecture, on the classical Greek playwright Euripides. It was a time of searching, of trying to find himself, of dropping the restrictions of a provincial, upper-middle-class ex-Jewish family, and of establishing the goals and aims he had outlined in his graduation essay at Trier when he was only seventeen.

Marx had plunged into the typical life of the nineteenth-century European students made famous by operettas of students in uniform, singing, dancing, drinking and seducing peasant girls. It was the kind of good living he was to maintain, though in a more stodgy form, until his death almost half a century later. But his years at Berlin were costly. His father, now ailing with tuberculosis, was called upon constantly to send more money. Heinrich Marx complained at one point that he had already sent Marx in a few months the equivalent of what he would himself earn in a year. Yet the demands went on, the bills piled up, the creditors appeared with their smiles and then their threats. This, too, was a pattern that Marx was to carry with him almost to the grave, this endless desperation over bills, which might have been curbed in his student years.

Heinrich Marx was unusually generous with his son. At one point he wrote, complaining about young Karl's endless requests, "Just as if we were made of money, in one year Your Highness has gone through almost 700 talers, contrary to any agreement or any custom, whereas the richest do not spend 500. But why?" There was no logical answer, of course. Young Marx would write back letters in which he couched his need for more money in terms his father considered abstract, philosophical, and transcendent. Heinrich Marx was forced to reply to these abstruse phases, "I am not going to keep on defending myself . . . on the paltry subject of money. . . . I occasionally reproach myself for having been much too weak in giving you your own way. We are now in the fourth month of the law year, and already you have had 280 talers. I have not yet earned that much this winter." In some specific terms, Heinrich Marx mentioned another student, eight years older than his son, who got by quite well on 180 to 200 talers a year, and he also pointed out that a Berlin town councilor received 800 talers a year. In the end, however, he told his son, who obviously wanted the money without the arguments, "Still you must always believe firmly that you have a place in the inmost recesses of my heart and that you are one of the strongest supports of my life."

A conflict had developed between the father and the son, which was waged on two unrelated levels, as if they were conversing in different languages. Most of what is known stems from a group of letters that have survived, one long letter from Karl to his parents, seventeen letters from the father to his son, and four from his mother and sister Sophie. Those from his father are believed to be the only letters Marx ever kept, and throughout his life he had such an intense feeling for his father that despite their basic conflict, Marx always carried his father's photograph, which was placed in his coffin by Engels.

Like most parents, Heinrich Marx saw his son as his extension in time—doing, completing, achieving the things he himself had never accomplished. "I should like to see in you what I myself might have become, if I had seen the light under such favorable auspices." Yet he was also careful not to try to direct his son into any particular career, which was unusual at a time of heavy parental control when children were not considered to have rights or opinions and were expected to follow the dictates of their elders. Whatever plans for a career Karl proposed—the law, teaching, or literary life—the father agreed to, although he was obviously baffled by the constant shift from one proposed livelihood to another. He was puzzled by the fragments of poems, a novel, and other literary works Karl sent him. Yet in his letters he tried to offer sensible advice about getting the material published. ("I have read your poem carefully, I confess to you frankly, my dear Karl, I don't understand it—either the real meaning or the general drift.") He advised his son in other areas: to train his voice to eliminate his Rhenish accent, not to wear himself out from overwork, and not to be lazy.

But the real crisis in his relationship with his father came when Karl openly announced his engagement to Jenny von Westphalen. The father tried to warn his son about the tremendous responsibilities he was taking on, implying that he would be marrying above himself and that he would endanger Jenny's own life. He counseled further that young Marx was not yet ready as a man and must establish himself first. "My dear Karl, at the risk of offending you, I must speak my mind in my own somewhat prosaic fashion. . . . She brings you an inestimable treasure—she demonstrates a self-denial. . . . But I beg and implore you, now that you really possess this treasure although everything is not yet smooth, to moderate these storms of passion." Beneath these questions was a fundamental fear, which he was able to state more candidly: "Sometimes I cannot drive away sad, ominous, fearful ideas when the thought suddenly creeps in: Does your heart match your head and your abilities? Does your heart really have room for the earthly but gentler feelings?" And then: "Do you think . . . that you will ever be capable of feeling a truly human, domestic happiness? . . ." "I cannot quite get rid of the idea that you are not free from egoism, that you have more of it than one needs for self-preservation." Heinrich Marx's worries came to the surface, the worries that this improvident son, unable to fix his mind on any one career, who wrote bits of oddities no intelligent man could fathom, was going to get himself bound by marital obligations without considering how these obligations were going to be fulfilled.

Young Marx finally answered his father's questions about what he was doing at the university, how he spent his time, what studies he was taking. The letter, dated November 10, 1837, is not particularly coherent. It is more anguished than explanatory, and it gives some indication of the turmoil and confusion he was experiencing. He begins by saying that a new world has opened up for him in many ways, yet he is depressed. He tries writing lyric poetry as a way out of his depression but it fails, and he turns to the study of law and of philosophy. The depth of his learning at this stage is amazing for, "Both [law and philosophy] were so interconnected that I examined Heineccius, Thibaut and the sources uncritically like a schoolboy and thus translated the first two books of Pandects into German and at the same time tried to elaborate a philosophy that would cover the whole field of law." He wrote three hundred pages of philosophical analysis before stopping, realizing "the falsity of the whole conception." He drove himself deeper into his studies, into philosophy, metaphysics, jurisprudence. He seemed to be working himself into a breakdown, and a doctor advised some rest in the country. Marx's brief excursion into a nearby village was the first time he had been outside of Berlin.

Next he studied Kant, Fichte, and Hegel, philosophers who are not commonly read today except perhaps in excerpt or summary. He wrote "a dialogue of about twenty-four pages entitled 'Cleanthes or the Starting-Point and Necessary Progress of Philosophy.' " During this time he had not had any word from Jenny for a year, for she believed that there should be no letters between them until their engagement was openly announced. This silence was depressing to Marx. Anger, frustration, and a sense of hopelessness overwhelmed him. "I ran like a madman around the garden beside the dirty waters of the Spee [a river in Berlin]." When he recovered from his siege, "I burnt all my poems and sketches for novels, etc., fancying that I could be completely free from them, which has at least not yet been disproved."

This letter—and I have only summarized it and quoted small sections—failed completely to communicate Karl's feelings to Heinrich Marx. The father could not understand what the son had written: words, phrases, sentences escaped him. The father could only try to write back about "life as it really is," and to express again his concern about the engagement to one of the noblest of young women from a very respectable family and his worries over a relationship which he saw as full of dangers and dismal prospects for his own child. Heinrich Marx beseeched his son to "exorcize all evil spirits, to banish all aberrations, make up for all shortcomings, and develop new and better

motives; make a wild young man into an orderly person, convert a negative genius into a genuine thinker, and make a dissolute ringleader into a sociable man."

And then, of course, there were the usual complaints about
money. But suddenly the conflict was to end. Heinrich Marx
had long been suffering from liver problems and tuberculosis.
On May 10, 1838, six months after his son's anguished letter,
he died.

The Struggle with Hegel   Though Marx had written his
father that he had "read fragments of Hegel's philosophy [and]
I did not care for its grotesque and rocky melody," he had, in
his unfinished essay on philosophy, attempted a synthesis of
certain basic themes. "Here are art and science," he told his
father, "which had become separate regained to some extent
their unity, and I vigorously set about the job itself, a philosophical and dialectical development of the divinity as it manifests
itself in idea-in-itself, religion, nature and history." This
densely stated sentence embodies the beginning of Hegel's
elaborate and convoluted philosophical system. Despite his uneasy state of mind, Marx studied Hegel and most of his disciples
from beginning to end.

For educated Europeans, particularly young Germans, Hegel was the pre-eminent thinker, philosopher, and intellectual
leader, who had broken through the limitations of past philosophy. At the university in Berlin there were two major schools
of Hegelians. The orthodox took certain of Hegel's mystical,
Christian-inspired concepts such as the "Absolute Idea" and
used them to vindicate the existing political system of the Prussian state, with its emphasis on the king as the focal point. The
Young Hegelians, also called the Left Hegelians, rejected the
relics of religious and political orthodoxy of Hegel's doctrines

and turned his methods to form a critique of religion and the state.

Hegel's beliefs are often abstruse and turgidly expressed. They can defy simplification and summary. Although they were of the utmost importance at the time, they have come down to us today in diluted and popular forms. What may seem like a commonsense observation, for example, that the present builds upon the past, that what happens today has its foundation in the events of yesterday, or that all aspects of a society bear some relationship to one another, was a revolutionary discovery for the Hegelians. Hegel saw the world as a totality in the process of continuous development and ascent from the lower to the higher, each age being on a better moral, intellectual, and material level than the preceding. He believed that development comes about through the struggle and resolution of internal contradictions. Each stage of development, which he labeled an affirmation, produced a challenge, an opposite or negative. The struggle between the two produced a synthesis, the negation of the negation, which in turn he called a new affirmation. This, briefly, is his famous dialectic, an endlessly repeated process.

Hegel saw too that seemingly unrelated subjects—for example, a nation's wars and its intellectual life—are pieces of the whole. Whatever happens, whatever develops, is but part of different aspects of a single great stream. He believed that at certain times conditions exist which must produce a certain type of music, art, mathematics, science, form of government, law, or any other human activity. All—whether folklore or higher mathematics, clothing or forms of warfare—are elements in a total "organic" development in the history of humanity, unfolding in his dialectic.

But this development, this dialectic, does not proceed smoothly. Hegel believed that life is a series of conflicts, of

The German philosopher Hegel was a key influence on Marx.

upheavals, crises, revolutions, unavoidable change, waste, and destruction. He stated that every process is one of necessary tension between incompatible forces straining against one another and by this conflict advancing their own development. In turn, out of each apparent solution there arise new conflicts because new forces appear, determined to assert themselves. These conflicts may not always be open nor on a massive scale; they may take place in the laboratory, or the arts, in people's minds, as well as on the battlefield. Two seeming truths in conflict may produce another truth, which in turn is challenged. This continual give and take, push and pull, absorption and resolution, challenge and response is all part of the dialectic. These principles he applied to human society.

But why and how did this dialectic take place? Hegel rejected the thesis of a supernatural force of the type espoused by Jews and orthodox Christians. He saw instead something he called the Divine Idea, the Absolute, or merely the Idea. He believed that the natural world as it existed, and humanity as well, are but manifestations of revelations of a cosmic spirit. This was a term used by other German philosophers of his age, but often vaguely and in different contexts. In general Hegel meant the Absolute as an organic entity, eternal, self-caused, spiritual; in some passages, however, it referred to a cosmic person or a "self-thinking thought," unknowable except to a few rare individuals through mystical insight.

It was the idea of the world and humanity as manifestations of the Absolute which the orthodox Hegelians saw embodied in church and state. Hegel himself said that Prussia was "the complete realization of the Spirit in existence . . . the Divine Idea in so far as it is existent on earth. The state was "what is rational in and for itself . . . the absolutely supreme phenomenal form of the Spirit." He dismissed the citizens of the state as the "so-called people." And he denounced a liberal teacher, a Professor Fries of Jena, for saying that, in a state where the universal mind is dominant, "life came from below, from the people." The limited monarchy of Prussia he viewed as the summit of the development of society. In specific terms, he meant that the king need only make some "improvements" to satisfy the middle classes in order to have the perfect state. And in a personal sense, he believed that his own philosophical system was the completion of human thought, that beyond it there could be nothing. He, Hegel, had capped human thought.

Hegel had died in 1831, leaving behind twenty volumes of dense and involuted reasoning. Marx was to draw upon it, at first wholeheartedly and then with increasing selection. He said later, "The mystification which dialectic suffers in Hegel's hands by no means prevents him from being the first to present its general form of working in a comprehensive and conscious manner. With him it is standing on its head. It must be turned right side up again, if you would discover the rational kernel within the mystical shell." And he openly avowed "myself the pupil of that mighty thinker." Though Marx rejected Hegel's supernatural phenomena, he held to the Hegelian view of the dialectic of history. Hegelianism may seem remote to us today, but in Marx's days at Berlin it was a living issue, and out of it came some basic concepts that were to serve Marx's purposes, as well as those of his future collaborator, Friedrich Engels, who came to Berlin a year later, in September, 1841, after Marx had left.

In Berlin Marx had come under the influence of a young Left Hegelian teacher named Bruno Bauer, who had also taught the course in Isaiah that Marx took one term. Bauer was to have a strong influence on Marx for a few years, but Marx would subsequently reject him. Bauer was in the midst of a controversy over religious questions. He had adopted the ideas of the writer David Friedrich Strauss, who had seen the Gospels as a collection of spontaneous myths expressing the aspirations of the early Christian communities. But in a two-volume *Life of Jesus,* published in 1835-36, Bauer stated that the Gospels were the product of a deliberate mythogenesis, and unlike Strauss, who accepted Christ as a historical figure who was raised to divinity by his followers, Bauer thought Christ was only myth, and the Gospels pure fiction. For these views Bauer was dismissed.

Bauer and the other Young Hegelians turned to the criticism of another sacrosanct subject, the state, and the dissension with the orthodox Hegelians lbecame political as well as religious. In this acrimonious atmosphere, Marx felt he could no longer follow an academic career. With Bauer's urging, he finished his doctoral thesis, and in April, 1841, submitted it to the philosophical faculty at the University of Jena, which was more liberal than Berlin. He received his doctorate a week later. Now there was nothing to do but to return to the relatively freer atmosphere of the Rhineland.

Here, in the closely grouped ancient cities of the Rhine— Bonn, Trier, and Cologne—he found himself among fellow liberals, many of whom had been recently at the university in Berlin. One of them was a young businessman named Moses Hess, who wrote to another friend, "You can prepare yourself to meet the greatest philosopher now living, perhaps the only one," adding, "Dr. Marx (for that is the name of my idol) is still quite a young man, about 24 years of age at the most, and he is about to deal the finishing stroke to medieval religion and politics. He combines the most profound philosophical seriousness with a cutting wit. Imagine for yourself Rousseau, Voltaire, Holbach, Lessing, Heine and Hegel [all prominent

intellectuals of the period] united in one person—and I say
united, not just thrown together, then you've got Dr. Marx."
With this kind of reputation, Marx was a highly popular and
even romantic figure among the Rhenish liberals. But, having
cast aside the idea of a post as a teacher, he had to find another
career. Presently one of the few jobs he was ever to hold in his
life was offered to him. In early 1842 he joined the staff of the
newly founded *Rheinische Zeitung,* a newspaper published in
Cologne. It had been founded by a group of wealthy liberals,
and its staff and contributors were drawn primarily from the
Left Hegelians of Berlin, among them Marx's future collaborator, Friedrich Engels.

Marx's articles, opinionated and biting, immediately became
popular, and by October of the same year he was made editor
of the paper. It was during this time that a basic change came
in his life. Marx was forced to face social and economic questions. Writing later he said:

> It was during the years 1842-43, as editor of the *Rheinische
> Zeitung,* that I found myself in the predicament of having to
> join in the discussion about so-called material interests. It was
> the negotiations of the Rhine Landtag regarding the theft of
> wood and the parcelling up of real estate, the official polemic
> concerning conditions among the Moselle peasants which Herr
> von Schaper (then President of the Rhine Province) launched
> against the *Rheinische Zeitung,* and finally the debates about
> free trade and protective tariffs that first caused me to occupy
> myself with economic questions.

It was this initial ignorance of economics that sent him to
restudy subjects he had dealt with earlier out of sympathy for
the people who were being oppressed or cheated by government, landowners, or industrialists. Marx had to admit that

The Chartists, an English proletarian movement, clashed often with the authorities in protesting working conditions.

originally he wrote many articles without adequate research. But whatever he studied, he was being led into communism, though he did not know it and fought the idea, for he considered himself a philosopher, somewhat out of place for the moment, and he had little interest in economics. But the time was ripe, ideas were rife, and the century, marked by both rapidly expanding material wealth and rapidly increasing poverty of the proletariat, was explosive. In a most Hegelian manner he had been thrust into the eye of the approaching revolution.

Communism was a widely discussed doctrine, but it was still to be formed and shaped. I won't examine Marx's many sources, but he was an omnivorous reader and scholar, and little escaped his attention. Virtually every communist thinker had his unique plan for establishing the perfect state, though many schemes overlapped. In general there were schools of communism which advocated state ownership of everything, and other schools which saw the perfect society composed of hundreds, even thousands, of miniature states. Then there were those who wanted a violent, immediate smashing of the existing state and of the current social structure, and those who wanted a slow evolution. And opposed to those who wanted some form of state were the anarchists, as they came to be called, who wanted no state at all. Some of the better-known thinkers were the following.

William Godwin (1756-1836), credited with being the father of anarchism and one of the first with a well-known and widely discussed program, advocated a stateless society of small property owners; he rejected the idea of any government at all or the right of anyone to hold large tracts of land. Godwin considered the power of the state as an evil. His contemporary in France, Gracchus Babeuf (1760-1797), the leader of the Union of Equals, however, thought social and economic equality could be attained only in a society without any private property; the state was to be the sole owner. Babeuf was executed for preparing for an armed uprising. Marx, deprecating the Babouvists as crude, uncivilized materialists, still appreciated them as champions of the workers and said they were the first examples of a communist party and the carriers of a new world order. One of the most important thinkers was F.C. Fourier (1772-1837), another Frenchman. He was a sharp critic of the social order, but his solution, which was a society of workers living in community houses, the phalanstères, became a reality only in the United States, where the best-known house, Brook Farm, near Boston, attracted Nathaniel Hawthorne, Margaret Fuller, and

Charles A. Dana; the latter, as an editor of the *New York Tribune,* was to hire Marx as a correspondent. Fourier expected that each phalanstère would be composed of workers in the same field; Brook Farm was a center for intellectuals. The United States, more than any other land, attracted utopian communities, many founded by immigrants from Europe. There were at least 178 such communities, according to known records, totalling, it is believed, hundreds of thousands of members. Among the better known are the Icarian communes of Texas and Iowa, Harmony and New Harmony, and the Oneida community.

Probably the most important voice to speak out early and intelligibly in the early nineteenth century was Pierre Joseph Proudhon, who believed in a peaceful transition to a perfect society. His central theme was that man should live in free association in an organization of social and national groupings, with no central state. This, of course, is anarchism, and to Proudhon goes the credit for using the term in its modern sense. Proudhon was at first one of Marx's friends; later Marx was to reject him as a reformist whose plan would aid the small producer and small land-owner but not the factory workers.

In general the utopian movements were based on a peaceful progress toward the perfect society, in which everyone would have enough of the world's goods and would contribute to the general welfare according to ability. In most of these plans, even the upper classes and the industrialists might have a role, if they subjected themselves to the rules of the cooperatives. In the 1840s Marx and Engels denounced such movements as socialist or anarchist, using the term communist for another, more radical, violent transformation of society, in which the workers would rise against the ruling classes and seize control of the machinery of the state and of industry as well. Marx was to take what he wanted from any movement, whether socialist, anarchist or communist, but from the beginning, his heart and mind were with the communists, and he was to give that movement the special character that has closely identified it with his name alone.

Marx took control of the *Rheinische Zeitung* with an iron hand. He accused some of the Berlin correspondents of having turned the weekly paper into a "docile organ." He said privately that he wanted "less vague reasoning, loud phrases, smugness and self-admiration, and more definiteness, more attention to concrete reality and more expert knowledge." At first he felt uneasy about "communist" doctrines introduced by some of his columnists into the paper. He worried that the censors might suppress it, and he was also concerned that the contributors "by their political romanticism, vainglory and boastfulness might compromise the success of the party of freedom." He said plainly, "I held the smuggling into incidental theatre reviews, etc., of communist and socialist dogmas, that is, of a new world view, to be unsuitable and indeed immoral, and that I desire quite a different and more profound discussion of communism if it were to be discussed at all."

When another paper accused the *Rheinische Zeitung* of communist sympathies, Marx replied:

> The *Rheinische Zeitung* does not even concede *theoretical validity* to communist ideas in their present form, let alone desires their practical realization, which it anyway finds impossible, and will subject these ideas to a fundamental criticism. . . . We are firmly convinced that the true danger does not lie in the practical attempt to carry out communist ideas, but in their *theoretical development;* for practical attempts, *even by the masses,* can be answered with a cannon as soon as they have become dangerous.

Although this was a very pragmatic and cautious point of view, shortly thereafter the secret police and the censors found even Marx's moderate position unacceptable. Liberal journalists presented a threat to the throne, so sanctified by Hegel's theory that it was the complete realization of the Spirit in existence. Censorship increased: sometimes an issue would come out so mutilated that Marx considered it hardly worth publishing. He was now fighting on two fronts, for he was also moving toward a complete break with the Young Hegelians. In January he wrote to a friend, Arnold Ruge: "I have become tired of hypocrisy, stupidity, gross arbitrariness, and of our bowing and scraping, dodging and hair-splitting over words." The same month Berlin imposed an even harsher censorship upon the paper, accusing it of hostility toward the state and church, and, among other things, of heaping abuse upon a foreign power. The power was Prussia's closest ally, Russia, the senior partner of the so-called Holy Alliance. The Czar's envoy to Berlin hoped to get the *Rheinische Zeitung* banned.

Marx could see that to proclaim liberal ideas in Germany was virtually impossible. Almost as a response to his problems, Ruge wrote to ask him if he would like to come to Paris to edit a new liberal journal that was being planned. And then Berlin announced that the *Rheinische Zeitung* was to be closed down: the last issue was to appear as of April 1, 1843. Marx wrote to Ruge accepting the offer, and resigned as editor of the *Rheinische Zeitung* on March 18. The new publication was to be called the *Deutsch-Französiche Jahrbücher* (the *German-French Annual*) and was to be written in German. Meanwhile Marx found that his efforts had not lacked appreciation. The Moselle wine growers, whose cause Marx had fought for, along with many other groups he had helped in the pages of the *Rheinische Zeitung,* drew up petitions to Berlin stating that the paper had

Jenny von Westphalen, after a painting made in the 1830s. She and Marx married in 1843 and then left Germany for Paris.

not spread false information, not slandered the state, but, in fact, had written nothing but the truth about the Rhineland.

The closing down of the *Rheinische Zeitung* was the act which drove Marx into a radical career. We cannot ever know if Marx would have become a communist if he had been allowed to remain as editor of this liberal but not actually dangerous Rhenish weekly. But now Marx realized that he had to face the world as it actually was. He turned back to Hegel to look for clues in philosophy, but the more he studied Hegel, the less he could accept Hegel's theory of the primacy of the state, although it was to be the workers' state that would replace the princely state. In his philosophy Marx was moving away from Hegel and was beginning to see people above all as social beings, products of historically rooted social relations.

While he was trying to work out his philosophical and intellectual position, he decided it was time to marry the very patient Jenny von Westphalen. Marx told a friend, "I can assure you without any romanticism that I am with all earnestness head over heels in love. I have already been engaged for over seven years and my bride has fought the hardest of all fights for me that have undermined her health." He told Ruge that he would be bringing Jenny to Paris with him: "I have quarreled with my family and, as long as my mother is alive, I have no right to my inheritance. Besides, I am engaged to be married, and I cannot and will not leave Germany without my fiancée."

A marriage contract, a formality common in Europe at the time, was signed, and on June 19, 1843, Marx and Jenny von Westphalen were married. The few months from the closing of the *Rheinische Zeitung* to the October of the same year are said to be the happiest of Marx's life, for after that he was to face unceasing hardship, worry, and privation. He and Jenny lived in the town of Kreuznach during this period, and with no worries on his mind, Marx could throw himself into his studies, filling five densely written notebooks, which came to be known as the Kreuznach Notebooks. He also kept up a heavy correspondence with many people, especially with Ruge about the new journal to be published in exile.

To prepare himself for his new life in Paris, Marx applied himself with his usual intensity to a study of French history and philosophy. Before leaving for France, Marx wrote to Ruge that he thought the paper should take a definite political attitude and comment on contemporary events and problems. This was a change from Marx's editorial position on the *Rheinische Zeitung*. Late in October Marx and his new wife settled in Paris, where he was to stay for almost eighteen months. Here his thinking would undergo its final transformation from the vestiges of liberalism to the development of a form of communism different from that of his predecessors and contemporaries. In Paris he began to focus clearly on the essential element in the struggle, the proletariat, the working people of Europe.

The first issue of the *Deutsch-Französiche Jahrbücher* appeared at the end of February, 1844. It contained a large number of articles by Marx, two pieces by Engels, whom he was just getting to know, some letters, verse, and articles by other well-known liberals and radicals of the time, and a selection of letters by Ruge, Feuerbach, and the Russian radical Mikhail Bakunin, who was to play a vital role in the coming rise of the communist movement. One of Marx's articles was a discussion of Hegel, a subject that by now must have become boring to a number of people. Another was entitled "On the Jewish Question," in which Marx tackled an issue that was to nag him throughout his life and to lead his friends, especially Engels, and his disciples in some strange directions.

The article was ostensibly in answer to his former teacher

and friend from Berlin, Bruno Bauer, who thought the only solution for the eternal plight of the Jews was emancipation from religion. But Marx saw the question not in religious, but in social and political, terms. He wrote: "Let us not seek the mystery of the Jew in his religion; let us rather seek the mystery of the religion in the actual Jews. . . . The emancipation from commerce and money, that is today from practical real Judaism, would be the self-emancipation of our time." Thus Marx was seemingly repeating the old medieval slander that the Jews were nothing but money-lenders and stockbrokers. Marx's writings have been interpreted in different ways by his disciples and his enemies. Some followers merely ignore his statements, others explain them away as being an objectionable and tasteless way of handling a serious problem, and still others see them as confirmation, by a Jew, of ancient prejudices.

Marx himself ignored his own Jewish ancestry, and Engels, who was a Christian, never mentioned Marx's Jewish background. Both men could make violent anti-Semitic remarks, and one of their favorite targets was the radical Ferdinand Lassalle. For a while Lassalle was their friend but he later became an enemy. Marx privately called Lassalle "Itsig," a pejorative name, and in his letters to Engels, "Yiddel Brown." Engels called Lassalle "a typical Jew from the Slav frontier," "a greasy Jew from Breslau," and "Oi, oi, the great Lassalle." Quite some time later (in 1862), Marx was particularly vituperative and in a letter to Engels described Lassalle as follows: "It is perfectly obvious from the shape of his head and the way his hair grows that he is descended from the Negroes who joined Moses on the journey out of Egypt, unless perhaps his mother or his grandmother had relations with a nigger."

Though Marx and Engels never spoke about his ancestry, Marx once remarked that "the traditions of all past generations weigh like a mountain on the minds of the living." One of Marx's earliest and best biographers, Franz Mehring, the founder of the Communist Party of Germany, believed Heinrich Marx had outgrown his Jewishness and that young Karl Marx had taken over this complete freedom from all Jewish influence. But an anti-Jewish attitude ran through his life. In discussing Jews or the "Jewish Question," he could write: "What is the mundane basis of Judaism? Practical needs: self-interest. What is the mundane cult of the Jews? Huckstering. What is the Jews' mundane god? Money."

2

The Making of
a Communist

In Paris Marx lived for the first time in his life among the
workers, the proletariat. Unfortunately, much as he could sympathize with the proletariat from a distance, he was unable to
strike up close relationships. He found the French workers
crude and unintelligent, yet he could see that they possessed a
certain unity and strength which enabled them to survive their
vicissitudes. "The brotherhood of man is no mere phrase with
them but a fact of life, and the nobility of man shines upon us

from their work-hardened bodies," Marx wrote in a notebook in 1844.

Even though Marx tried to get close to these workers, attending their meetings, sitting with them in their cafés, he never fully made contact. He was, in fact, virtually isolated, almost a recluse at this period. Except for the Ruges, with whom he and Jenny lived in a kind of commune, he saw few Germans, even though Paris was then a great center for Germans in forced or voluntary exile, harboring a colony of almost 85,000 artisans, intellectuals, and liberals. He spent much of his time in study. Ruge described him to Feuerbach as follows:

> He reads a great deal; he works with extraordinary intensity and has a talent for criticism, which occasionally degenerates into abuse. However, he never finishes anything; he is always breaking off and then plunging into an infinite ocean of books. . . . He may well have been born to be a scholar and a writer, but as a journalist he is a complete failure.

Aside from Ruge, Marx's closest friends at this period were Moses Hess, Mikhail Bakunin, and the poet Heinrich Heine, who announced in a poem, "I have boarded a ship with new comrades." Heine, unlike the others, was not a communist but was attracted by his companions' atheism; later he was to become something of a deist.

Marx Looks at Capitalism in Theory   From April through August of 1844, Marx made a concentrated study of a number of European philosophers and economists, which included not only his old philosophical adversary Hegel but also Feuerbach and the growing school of English economists, especially Adam Smith, David Ricardo, James Mill, and many others whose names and ideas are rarely remembered. Economics was a new field of study for the scholar: the rapid developments in the world were easily apparent to a number of perceptive men in Europe, for in their own lifetimes they were witnesses to marked economic, social, and political changes, and many thinkers were trying to find common patterns. When handcrafts and cottage industries, for example, were replaced by high-speed machines, the result was greater profits for the owners and the impoverishment of the workers. This type of problem attracted much concern. Some, like the Physiocrats of late eighteenth-century France, wanted to divert the new industrial movements into an economic science based upon agriculture rather than trade. The Physiocrats advocated a lessening of taxation. They believed that since people are intelligent, virtuous, and reasonable, an enlightened self-interest makes it as easy to build as to destroy.

The dominant theory that was to develop was that of laissez-faire or free trade, which proposed unregulated commerce that was unhampered by quotas or tariffs, in the belief that competition within nations and between nations is the best form of regulation. One of the leading exponents of laissez-faire was Adam Smith (1723-1790), who believed in a form of capitalism that was raw, crude, aggressive, and without mercy, an idea which still has a great appeal to many businessmen in these days of complex government regulations. Smith was the first major thinker to grapple with the concept of the accumulation of wealth and the production of goods, which in turn produced more wealth or capital. Smith was by nature an optimist and his famous work, *An Inquiry into the Nature and Causes of the Wealth of Nations,* had an air of success and good living, at least for the class that was obtaining the capital.

Smith believed that economic progress results when there is a minimum of interference by the state, regulation and control coming by competition in the free market. The person who could beat his competitors with lower prices, higher quality, better distribution, better access to raw materials, and the best methods of production would be successful. And the success of a business meant the enrichment of society and thus of all people. But Smith noted that there were two major groups making up this society, and he could easily "foresee which of the two parties must upon all ordinary occasions have the advantage of the dispute." As he succinctly pointed out, "We have no acts of Parliament against combining to lower the price of work [that is, of wages paid], but many against combining to raise it." Consequently, while the men at the top got richer, the workers could only become poorer. The fault in such a system was this:

> A man must always live by his work, and his wages must at least be sufficient to maintain him. They must even upon most occasions be somewhat more, otherwise it would be impossible for him to bring up a family, and the race of such workmen could not last beyond the first generation.

Smith's major concern was not humanitarian—the plight of the worker—but economic: how long would the cheap labor pool last for the capitalist? It seemed to be an iron law of nature, an economic nature, that the worker would exist only on the bare survival level. This was to be eventually challenged by Marx, once he had been able to digest the sheer horror of a theory that put the wealth of the few above the misery of the many.

Smith also discovered the law of surplus value, so important in Marx's later thinking, although Marx was to refashion it according to his own views. Smith pointed out that surplus value is created by any type of social labor—from rents, profits, or interest—as well as from the product of the workers' unpaid or extra labor. Marx said that Smith had confused surplus value with profit, and it was the workers' productivity alone—and nothing else—that produced surplus value.

Ricardo (1772-1823) added further to Smith's iron laws of capital and labor. He pointed out that as profits rose and capital accumulated, population would increase, and since there was only a limited amount of land, there would be an increase in rent as the demand grew. Industrialists and landowners would prosper but the masses would not, for they have nothing to sell but their labor. A famous passage by Ricardo puts the role of the worker into clear-cut terms:

> Labour, like all other things which are purchased and sold, and which may be increased or diminished in quantity, has its natural and its market price. The natural price of labour is that price which is necessary to enable the labourers, one with another, to subsist and perpetuate the race, without either increase or diminution.

"Iron laws" like this, Ricardo found, would lead to the inevitable impoverishment of the people and the progressive enrichment of those who own and control the natural means of production. He noted, too, that there would be an inevitable conflict between the people who worked for wages and those who demanded profits and an accumulation of capital. Ricardo presented these observations as objective facts. His detachment and lack of compassion for the masses of people brought the accusation from the writer and artist John Ruskin that he was a cold-blooded stockbroker totally unconcerned about the misery he foresaw the common man enduring for eternity.

These men had a profound influence upon Marx, and he made extensive notes and commentaries about their ideas. His incomplete and fragmentary manuscripts from this brief period, known as the *Economic and Philosophic Manuscripts of 1844,* were not published until 1959 in Moscow. They contain his first enunciation of the important concept of "alienation," which he had derived from Hegel and Feuerbach and had used in a new context, that of its application to labor. Hegel had spoken of a world of the spirit alienated from itself. Feuerbach saw the individual alienated from the common natural properties shared by all people. Marx went further and found that individuals' social lives, their working conditions, and their relationships with other people were all alien and hostile. He believed that alienation was the direct outcome of the private property system. And alienation in the sphere of economics led to other forms of alienation.

Under bourgeois capitalism, "Man is made alien to man," for in making something, the worker produces another power, the product, which enriches the capitalist and impoverishes the worker. The products of labor go to the capitalist who owns the means of production and not to the worker who creates the product. And capital is private property created by another person's labor. Working conditions and the act of working become the worker's curse—"external to the worker," not part of "his essential being." Thus the worker does not affirm himself but denies himself, does not feel content but unhappy. Factory work is a kind of bondage or servitude to which most workers are tied for life. The spiritual side is lost, and pleasures are reduced to purely animal functions, like eating and drinking. The worker is himself only when he does not work, and when he works, he is not himself.

Such is the thesis of Marxian alienation, which was to be a basic concept in his writings in the future. It was one that the workers of Europe could easily understand, and they could accept Marx's teachings that the emancipation of the workers meant "universal human emancipation."

As Marx pursued his studies, he became more and more committed to communism, calling for an "uprising of the proletariat." Though he had once accepted Hegel almost wholeheartedly, Marx now condemned him, but he still employed Hegelian themes and concepts in his attacks. Where Hegel believed in the supremacy of the state over the family and civil society, Marx claimed that the contrary was true: that the state could exist only on the basis of the family and society. To Marx the rights of the people were paramount, for the state is an abstraction, and the people alone are concrete. They are the real state, and therefore monarchy is wrong because it subordinates the people. In a democracy, on the other hand, the constitution belongs not to the state but to the people. "Man does not exist because of law but law exists because of man." In a true democracy, said Marx, borrowing from his French contemporaries, who had long since proposed the idea, "the political state disappears." It is only when private and public interests coincide and remain so, that it is possible to speak of true democracy. He was later to call this concept "the classless society."

He seemed at a turning point. He wrote, "To be radical is to grasp things by the root. For man the root is man himself." Marx discounted religion because it did not put man first.

> The criticism of religion ends with the doctrine that man is the supreme being for man. It ends with the categorical imperative to overthrow all those conditions in which man is an abased, enslaved, abandoned, contemptible being.

He then turned to the concept of the proletariat, the "classless class," which is the root of society, out of which the new

world will be formed. This class is not to be another class of civil
society but

> A class which is the dissolution of all classes, a sphere of society
> which has a universal character because its sufferings are univer-
> sal, and which does not claim a particular redress because the
> wrong which is done to it is not a particular wrong but wrong
> in general . . . which is, in short, a total loss of humanity and
> which can only redeem itself by a total redemption of humanity.
> This dissolution of society is the proletariat.

As a German, Marx saw salvation coming from Germany
and the Germans:

> The proletariat is only beginning to form itself in Germany, as
> a result of the industrial movement. For what constitutes the
> proletariat is not naturally existing poverty, but poverty artifi-
> cially produced. . . . In Germany no type of enslavement can
> be abolished unless all enslavement is destroyed. Germany,
> which likes to get to the bottom of things, can only make a
> revolution which upsets the whole order of things. The emanci-
> pation of Germany will be an emancipation of man.

Marx stated further that "philosophy is the head of this
emancipation and the proletariat is its heart." Marx the radical,
Marx the revolutionary, the sworn enemy of the past, the
enemy of the state and of the bourgeoisie, was now in the the
midst of his own complete radicalization. Up to this point he
had been known as a liberal journalist of biting and satirical
views, whose advocacy of democracy had enraged the censors
and the police. But now he was becoming the enemy not only
of repression but also of liberal reform. There could be no
halfway station in his world, no compromise with the world or
even in his personal life. Before him lay years of hardship, of
penury and insult, of little acclaim, for a cause that only he and

Engels and Jenny Marx and a few friends saw with equal clarity.

Marx and Engels Join Forces   It was in Paris that Marx and Engels became friends, after an unproductive meeting earlier in Cologne. In a sense, Engels had been Marx's shadow for years, following him from Berlin to Cologne to Paris. They had already exchanged letters, and Engels had sent him articles from Berlin for the *Rheinische Zeitung.*

Engels was two years Marx's junior, the member of a well-to-do family of German textile mill owners from Barmen in the Rhineland. He had eight brothers and sisters, the brothers all joining their father in the family mills and the sisters marrying men in the industry. One of Marx's daughters was to write later that "no son born into such a family ever struck so entirely different a path from it." Young Engels was a misfit, rejecting not only the textile industry as a career—although sheer necessity forced him to work in the family mills for a living for a number of years—but also his parents' religion and middle-class morals. Like Marx, Engels was raised as a Lutheran, but he protested that the church was bigoted and narrow.

In grammar school he received a good grounding in chemistry and physics and began to develop his extraordinary talent for languages. He was by nature a brilliant scholar and his genius led him to observe that his school was deficient in the teaching of Greek, Latin, and mathematics; the best he could say about the teachers was that they were "highly skilled bookkeepers." His rebellious attitude brought about his transfer to a Lutheran boarding school where his father and the headmaster thought the secluded way of life would lead him to "a certain degree of independence" and help him overcome "a disturbing thoughtlessness and lack of character." At this boarding school his character developed along lines that, strangely enough, pleased both adults and the student himself.

Young Engels studied history, Greek, Latin, and German classical literature. He wrote music, became a skilled artist and filled many notebooks with drawings of historical themes—Carthage, Jerusalem, Thermopylae, the Egyptian pyramids and Sphinx, Babylonian warriors, and Hindu and Greek architecture. He translated Homer, Euripides, Virgil, Horace, Livy, and Cicero from the Greek and Latin and was learned enough to write a poem in classical Greek, "The Single Combat of Eteocles and Polynices." His teachers described him as a modest, open-hearted, and friendly boy with the commendable intention of getting a good education. However, Engels privately labeled the school a "prison," and as Vladimir Ilyich Lenin, one of his later disciples, wrote, he "had come to hate autocracy and the tyranny of bureaucrats while still at high school."

In 1837, when he considered that his son was properly educated, the senior Engels took young Friedrich out of school and brought him into the family business at Barmen as an apprentice. Somehow, amid the whir of the spinning jennies, young Engels found time to continue his study of history, philosophy, literature, and languages and to write poetry. He became such an accomplished, though unwilling, businessman that the next year, for further experience, he was passed on to the mills of a family friend in Bremen, a large seaport in western Germany. Bremen was an important commercial center, trading with all parts of the world, and Engels soon picked up Italian, Spanish, Portuguese, English, and Dutch. He also continued his private studies in several fields and wrote musical pieces in the manner of Beethoven, then considered to be a modern composer. Engels also developed his athletic skills and became an expert horseman, swimmer, fencer, and skater.

His expanding interests led him further afield into social problems. He was only eighteen when he wrote two unsigned articles entitled "Letters from Wuppertal," which were published in a Rhenish newspaper. Engels attacked the middle-class bigotry of the people of Barmen, but his special point was the abysmal social conditions in the city and the wide gulf between the workers and the factory owners.

> Terrible poverty prevails among the lower classes, [he wrote] particularly the factory workers in Wuppertal; syphilis and lung diseases are so widespread as to be barely credible; in Eberfield alone [another town], out of 2,500 children of school age, 1,200 are deprived of education and grow up in the factories. . . . The wealthy manufacturers have a flexible conscience, and causing the death of one child more or less does not doom a pietist's soul to hell, especially if he goes to church every Sunday. For it is a fact that the church-goers among the factory owners treat their workers worst of all.

The articles created a lot of controversy, for the factory owners were not accustomed to criticism.

Meanwhile Engels turned to the books that were also attracting other young German intellectuals, especially David Strauss's *Life of Jesus* and Hegel's works, which Marx, halfway across Germany, was also reading. Strauss's work led Engels to a complete rejection of religion. And he found Hegel's *History of Philosophy,* which taught a continual ascendant movement to higher and more mature social forms, the basis for ideas he was to develop. Where the reactionaries, the "mandarins of retrogression," saw nothing in history but a repetition of the past, history, in Engels's view, moved forward continually. Old ideas, he said, will be crushed "under the admantine foot of forward moving time." Engels's writing was much clearer than

Marx's, more precise and penetrating. Where Marx would become involved in endless philosophical asides, Engels got right to the core of the matter. In an article attacking the chauvinist attitudes of the Germans themselves, he wrote that the outlook of the "Germanophiles was philosophically without foundation since it held that the entire world was created for the sake of Germans and the Germans themselves had long since arrived at the highest state of evolution."

Engels produced a series of articles, mature in thought and concept, analyzing current problems in the light of Hegelian dialectic but rejecting Hegel's political conservatism. He attacked the nobility for their unashamed chauvinism, their contempt for other nations, and their hatred for the democratic principles of the French Revolution. He thought the German princes were forcing their people back to the Middle Ages.

Then, in March, 1841, his apprenticeship in Bremen having been completed, he returned to the parental home in Barmen. But the life of a provincial city had no appeal, so Engels set off on a tour of Switzerland and Italy, preparatory to settling down for a while in Berlin, where he intended to enter the army and also to attend the university. He reached the capital in September and joined an artillery brigade quartered near the university. Military life was easy, and Engels found adequate time to take courses in various subjects. Almost immediately he became involved in the disputes between the orthodox Hegelians and the Left Hegelians. He quickly began to move toward a more radical position based on Hegelian doctrines. His mind was inquisitive and quick, and he was able to absorb the most involved aspects of Hegel's thought as he moved further and further into a political and philosophical radicalism. Still Engels was trying to get the basic themes sorted out, as in this extract of his work at the time.

The Free, a group of Young Hegelians, engage in one of their frequent arguments. The cartoon is by Engels, a member.

A sketch by Engels shows a pair of Prussian bourgeoisie, obsequiously approaching Kaiser Friedrich Wilhelm IV for favors.

> Up to now, all philosophy has made it its task to understand the
> world as rational. What is rational is, of course, also necessary,
> and what is necessary must be, or at least become, real. This is
> the bridge to the great practical results of modern philosophy.
> . . . Only *that* freedom is genuine which contains necessity.
> . . . The conclusion of modern philosophy . . . is that reason
> cannot possibly exist except as mind, and that mind can only
> exist in and with nature, and does not somehow lead a life apart,
> in separateness from it, God knows where.

He could also be more direct, for he saw that the older
generation of Hegelians was using the great philosopher to
serve the king of Prussia. He attacked the Prussian aristocracy
as well as the German radical bourgeoisie, who, he said, were
actually supporting the nobles and not the masses in the making
of history. He was confident, however, that progress would win
the ultimate victory over reaction. "Let us fight and bleed, look
undismayed into the grim eyes of the enemy and hold out to the
end! . . . The day of great decision, of the battle of nations, is
approaching, and victory must be ours!"

Arnold Ruge wrote Engels congratulating him on his ideas,
addressing him as "Doctor of Philosophy." Engels answered,
"I am not a Doctor and cannot ever become one. I am only a
merchant and a Royal Prussian artillerist, so kindly spare me
that title." He felt that his friends and readers were overestimat-
ing his accomplishments and wrote a friend in 1842 that he had
decided to give up literary work for a time.

> I am young and self-taught in philosophy. I have learnt enough
> to form my own viewpoint and, when necessary, to defend it,
> but not enough to be able to work for it with success and in the
> proper way. All the greater demands will be made on me be-
> cause I am a 'travelling agent' in philosophy and have not
> earned the right to philosophize by getting a doctor's degree.

But his writings, in various newspapers and pamphlets, had attracted wide attention. He was noticed not only in Germany but in Poland and Russia and was described as an outstanding contemporary philosopher.

No matter what their son's reputation might be among intellectuals, to the Engels family his chief obligation was to work in mills, although on a managerial level. Engels was packed off to a family mill in Manchester, England, and apparently he saw no other course since he was only twenty. However, on his way to England, he took the opportunity to stop off at Cologne, where Marx had just become editor of the *Rheinische Zeitung.* This was their first meeting; though they had both been in Berlin, Marx had left before Engels arrived. However, they had friends in common, among them many of the Left Hegelians in Berlin, and in Cologne, Moses Hess, the radical businessman. They had much to share, but Engels still retained his connections with the Berlin Young Hegelians, although his attitudes on social problems were more advanced than Marx's. Engels recalled toward the end of his life that this first meeting was "rather frigid."

"Marx," he wrote, "had meanwhile gone against the Bauers, that is, he opposed the idea that the *Rheinische Zeitung* should be chiefly a vehicle for theological propaganda, atheism, etc. instead of one of political discussion and action. . . . And since I corresponded with the Bauers I was regarded as their ally, while I, too, had been made suspicious of Marx by them." From Cologne Engels went on to Manchester, where he was to take the final step that led to his radicalization.

Manchester was the biggest city in southern Lancashire and the center of England's textile industry. It had the immense population of 400,000 people, mostly composed of mill workers, a small middle class, and above them the mill owners and members of other business enterprises. A large section of the old town, which was heavy with smoke and dirt and riven with narrow, twisting lanes and alleyways, consisted of the workers' quarters, slums of the most ferocious degradation. Engels arrived in Manchester in December of 1842, presented himself to the family representatives, and began working. He was to spend twenty-one months exploring these dank alleys, much of this time in the company of an Irish working girl, Mary Burns.

Engels's relationship with Mary Burns has provided the revolution with one of its many minor scandals. Miss Burns was a worker in the mills of Engels and Engels, attending a machine called a "self-actor." The official biography of Engels prepared by the Institute of Marxism-Leninism in Moscow states bluntly and incorrectly that, "Over the years their friendship grew into deep attachment and love," adding, "Mary became Engels's wife," a fact unknown to anyone else, including the Marxes, who literally turned their backs to Engels's companion when he brought her to a communist meeting in Brussels. Most Marxists and Communist literature ignore the Engels-Burns association, presenting Engels as virtually a celibate.

Miss Burns is described by people who met her as lively, sharp-witted and good-natured, and above all, independent, for she refused to give up her job in the Engels factory no matter how much he begged her; however, she accepted a house from him in a Manchester suburb, and lived there with her sister Lizzie. Both women were deeply involved in the cause of Irish freedom, and introduced Engels to their country's rebel leaders. The proletarian birth of his companion seemed to have disturbed Engels, for he developed the delusion that she was actually the descendant of the Scottish poet Robert Burns; he wasted much time in trips to Scotland and Ireland trying to trace the relationship.

The communists themselves disapproved of the liaison. Stephan Born, one of the original members of the Communist League, expressed open approval of Frau Marx's "intransigent" attitude towards Mary Burns. He also added a sensible comment of his own, for he felt that Engels's liaison insolently insulted the workers by justifying "the reproach so often made against the rich sons of manufacturers that they are in a position to press the daughters of the people into the service of their pleasures." (Born, who was to serve with valor in the revolutions of 1848, was soon denounced by Marx for preaching reformism and conciliation and being a petty bourgeois opportunist, all forms of heresy to Marx. What he had done was found a rather successful Workers Brotherhood in Berlin independent of Marx's control.)

Much later, in 1863, when Mary Burns died, Engels transferred his romantic affections to Lizzie Burns. He soon retired from business and moved to London with Lizzie, and he did marry her, on her deathbed, in 1879, to please her. But when the Marxes, especially Frau Marx and her daughters came to visit Engels in his home at Regent's Park Road, Engels would send Lizzie out shopping, with money for a drink or two at a pub and a ride through the park in a hansom cab.

It was the Burns girls who, in the early 1840s, showed him proletarian life in its rawest form. He was to write of Manchester, "I know it as intimately as my own native town, more intimately than most of its residents know it." He climbed over the garbage in the streets, visited the workers in the crowded cellars, made notes of what the people ate and drank and of the patent medicines they consumed (for some of them contained opium), learned about their sex habits, saw their early deaths, watched the children waste away. He wrote five articles for the *Rheinische Zeitung* about the conditions of the working people in England and the Chartist political movement many of them followed, and then he turned to work on a book, *The Condition of the Working Class in England in 1844.*

His descriptions of the life of the workers is graphic, sickening.

> The cottages are old, dirty and of the smallest sort, the streets uneven, fallen into ruts and in part without drains or pavements; masses of refuse, offal and sickening filth lie among standing pools in all directions, the atmosphere is poisoned by the effluvia from these, and laden and darkened by the smoke of a dozen tall factory chimneys. A horde of ragged women and children swarm about here, as filthy as the swine that thrive upon the garbage heaps and in the puddles.
>
>   . . . These pale, lank, narrow-chested, hollow-eyed ghosts, whom one passes at every step, these languid, flabby faces, incapable of the slightest energetic expression, I have seen in such numbers only in London.

He describes a dead woman covered with feathers because the coverlet had come apart.

> The feathers stuck so fast over the whole body that the physicians could not examine the corpse until it was cleaned, and then found it starved and scarred from the bites of vermin. Part of the floor of the room was torn up, and the hole used by the family as a privy.

Elsewhere he describes sixteen people living in a cellar with their pigs, and a railway being built through a cemetery where the newly buried bodies were not removed when the piles were driven into the graves. He describes the misery of the knife grinders, who died early from the dust of the knives they sharpened.

Dr. Knight has often told grinders who came to him with the first symptoms of asthma that a return to grinding means certain death, but with no avail. He who is a grinder falls into despair, as though he sold himself to the devil.

"Immorality among young people seems to be more prevalent in Sheffield [the great cutlery center] than anywhere else," he also wrote.

The younger generation spend the whole of Sunday lying in the street tossing coins or fighting dogs, go regularly to the gin palace. . . . Early, unbridled sexual intercourse, youthful prostitution, beginning with persons of fourteen to fifteen years, is extraordinarily frequent in Sheffield. Crimes of a savage and desperate sort are of common occurrence; one year before an investigating commissioner's visit, a band, consisting chiefly of young persons, was arrested when about to set fire to the town, being fully equipped with lances and inflammable substances.

He talks too of the London seamstresses, who live in tiny garrets and huddle together like animals trying to keep warm.

Here they sit bent over their work, sewing from four or five in the morning until midnight, destroying their health in a year or two and ending in an early grave, without being able to obtain the poorest necessities of life meanwhile.

He writes about child labor—children as young as five were employed sixteen hours a day and once he found a child of two working in a lace factory. The employment of children must be forbidden —"It is clearly unjust." And so Engels continued to explore the dark recesses of the English social structure, revealing the poverty and ill treatment of the workers and the hypocrisy of the owners. It was, he wrote, "the social war, the war of each against all." He added, "Society is already in a state of visible dissolution. . . . The enemies are dividing gradually into two great camps—the bourgeoisie on the one hand, the workers on the other." He warned, even predicted, that "the decisive battle between bourgeoisie and proletariat is approaching. . . . The only possible solution is a violent revolution, which cannot fail to take place. . . . The war of the poor against the rich will be the bloodiest ever waged." *The Condition of the Working Class in England in 1844* was published a year after the date in its title, and the "war" that Engels prophesied took place in 1848.

Meanwhile, his apprenticeship in the family factory in Manchester had been completed. His father told him that he was to return home, not knowing that his son had also served another apprenticeship as a radical thinker. At the end of August, 1844, Engels stopped off at Paris to try another meeting with Marx. This time they had more in common. Engels had rejected the Young Hegelians and other "radical bourgeois" acquaintances, and Marx had moved rapidly into communism. They had reached a common point.

They spent ten days together discussing theoretical and practical problems. "I have not been again in so happy and humane a mood as during the ten days I spent with you," Engels wrote to Marx from Bremen. Marx had introduced Engels to the editors of a new radical journal in Paris called *Vorwärts,* which, after a vague beginning, had become an organ of revolutionary and communist propaganda. The editors immediately put into print two articles Engels had with him about social problems in England. Engels outlined the industrial upheaval and the emergence of the proletariat. "Who really rules England?" he asked. "Property rules. The middle class and property rule; the poor man has no rights, is oppressed and flayed, the Constitution disowns him and the law maltreats him." With Marx, he began a pamphlet against the Young Hegelians, now their common enemies, with emphasis on Marx's former teacher, Bruno Bauer and his brothers Edgar and Heinrich, who were also Hegelians.

Engels continued on to Barmen, and Marx turned the pamphlet into a full-length book. It was called *The Holy Family*, mocking the Bauers, but it was not a biography. It was a full-scale analysis of the history of philosophy from the seventeenth century to the 1840s. The work, which is ponderous and yet makes poor jokes and puns, is an attempt at using the technique of dialectic. Analyzing the nature of the antagonistic contradiction between the middle class and the proletariat, Marx states that the internal structure consists of a conservative and a revolutionary side, where "within this antithesis the private owner is . . . the conservative side, the proletariat the destructive side." He emphasizes that the contending forces are irreconcilable. Thus, the only possibility is that the proletariat must emerge in control at the end, for such are the forces of history. " 'History' is not a person apart, using man as a means for its own particular aims; history is nothing but the activity of man pursuing his aims." The proletariat is determined by socioeconomic factors. The living conditions of the working class "sum up all the conditions of life in society today in all their inhuman acuity. . . . The proletariat executes the sentence that private property pronounced on itself by begetting the proletariat." Consequently the proletariat is bound to destroy capitalist society.

Meanwhile, as Marx was finishing *The Holy Family*, which was published in Frankfurt in March, 1845, the French government was having second thoughts about the sizeable colony of German radicals within its borders. The Prussian ambassador in Paris had been trying to persuade the French that these men

were preaching regicide, that they were in favor of assassinating
King Friedrich Wilhelm IV. The Prussians kept up their pres-
sure; *Vorwärts* was closed down in January, 1845; and Marx,
along with a small group of others, among them the Russian
radical Mikhail Bakunin, was given expulsion orders. But
where was he to go? To return to Germany was impossible. He
ruled out one country after another and finally decided that
Brussels, the capital of neighboring Belgium, might be the least
inhospitable city of all. He left Paris for Brussels on February
3, followed by Jenny and their first baby; Jenny had to sell the
remnants of their furniture to pay for her passage. This new seat
of exile, Marx hoped, would be not too far from both his con-
tacts in Germany and his friends in Paris. The Marxes were to
remain in Belgium for three years; during this period Marx did
some of his best and most creative work. Although he had
promised the Belgian government that he would not become
involved in politics or write about political problems, it was
impossible for him to abstain. The Belgian police and German
agents kept a watch on him.

Belgium was one of the most economically and industrially
advanced nations in Europe at that time, with well-developed
industries not only in textiles but also in mining and engineering. Manual labor was being replaced by large-scale machine
production. It was a perfect example of the kind of bourgeois-
capitalistic society that Marx and Engels were in the process of
analyzing and denouncing: the workers suffered a fourteen-
hour day; wages were low; there was much exploitation of
women and children at low wages, and unemployment. At the
same time the great industrialists boasted of tremendous economic prosperity. Though a liberal constitution had been
granted to the people, the right to vote was restricted to the one
percent of the population which held property.

The Marxes took up residence in a workers quarter, and soon Engels joined them, having reached the end of his patience with his family at Barmen. Brussels, like Paris, was full of exiles; some were working men and artisans who found the city a better place to make a living than their homelands, but most were intellectuals, liberals and radicals who sought a freer atmosphere. Though Marx attracted a number of Polish, French, Belgian, Russian, and Italian socialists and radicals to his home, most of his friends were emigrant Germans. The Marxes' household was increased during this period by two more children, a second daughter, Laura, and a son, Edgar, plus a country girl named Helene Demuth, nicknamed Lenchen, who was sent to Frau Marx by the von Westphalens as a kind of bonded servant. Lenchen must have been an unusual person, for she took over the running of the Marx home and family and stayed through the abrasive periods which were to follow, scraping up bits of money for food and taking their clothes to the pawnship when their credit was exhausted.

But from now on there was to be no compromise for Marx. He was approaching his late twenties, and the tenor of his life was becoming clear: he was a communist. There was no question of his finding a job to support his wife and children and servant. There was no goal but to pursue his course to the end no matter what happened, to forge the doctrine of the revolution both philosophically and realistically. While his mind could soar into the most abstruse philosophical problems on one hand, on the other it could seek the means by which to destroy his enemies in the most ruthless manner possible.

The Gnawing of the Mice   It was an age when romanticism ran rampant among the middle and upper classes. Imagination, intuition, the supremacy of the individual over society, liberation from conventional restrictions, stress upon emotion for its own sake, especially in poetry, literature, music, art, and architecture, were exalted. The romantic poet believed he had no responsibilities except to himself and his art, an attitude that found more prosaic expression among the new industrialists with their expanding factories and increasing wealth. The romantic rebel against the world enjoyed a symbol in the poet Lord Byron, who joined the Greeks in revolt against the Turks, only to lose his life. It was an act that was to foreshadow the tragic sacrifices of western intellectuals a century later in support of the Loyalist forces in the Spanish Civil War. And, as part of this unbridled romanticism, a new vocation arose, that of the professional revolutionary, the man who made a career out of risking his life in the cause of a better world.

For Marx, all such uncontrolled display of wild emotion, no matter what cause it served, was bourgeois vanity and stupidity. He assumed a matter-of-fact "scientific" attitude. ("Science" and "scientific" became catchwords in the Marxist vocabulary, for he was in the process of reducing hitherto untamed forces to manageable laws.) The only emotion Marx allowed himself was sarcasm against the enemies of the working class. To him it was but a question of applying correct principles, which he was in the process of discovering, to the dialectic of history. Out of the dialectic would come the better, more democratic, communist world he saw as inevitable. He could talk to the workers in the Belgian cafés, but he was not an inflammatory or inspired speaker and could not arouse them. He could analyze their problems, suggest aims and goals, but he could not lead them. He was anything but a dynamic leader, since his manner was brusque, matter-of-fact, sarcastic, and even hostile to those whose situation he was attempting to ameliorate. Even though Marx and Engels made a pretense of preferring the company of workers, they apparently felt uncomfortable with them, for in their private conversations the workers were "roughnecks" and "louts." (Their term for the bourgeoisie was "petticoats.")

They both threw themselves into a flood of writings—pamphlets, essays, reviews, volumes of notebooks. A large number of their works was never published, because either they were never finished or they were unsatisfactory to publishers or to Marx. One of Marx's major efforts in Brussels was a group of eleven statements entitled *Theses on Feuerbach,* which, though extremely short, was, according to Engels, "the first document in which is laid out the brilliant germ of the new world outlook." It is in this work that Marx coined his famous phrase, "religion is the opium [or opiate] of the people." Feuerbach comes off better than most of Marx's opponents. He is praised for his outlook on religion, which he stated was a form of escape. But Feuerbach is accused of not seeing that it is the pain of the material world that drives people to religion. Marx says in answer to Feuerbach that such ideas and beliefs as religion have no validity of their own. The true convictions of an individual or of a society are expressed in their acts, not in words. Belief and act are one, said Marx, otherwise they are lies. And, "Philosophers have previously offered various interpretations of the world. Our business is to change it." The pamphlet was not published during Marx's lifetime (Engels found it later after his death), but it was another step in clarifying his thinking.

A second important work, also unpublished except for some fragments, was the massive *The German Ideology,* a collaboration with Engels. They worked on it during 1846 and 1847, mostly at night, when they were freed from the daily chore of handling their revolutionary colleagues. This too is a seminal work in the development of their thought. Like much of their work, it began as an attack on other philosophers, German as

Friedrich Engels, in the 1840s, when he first met Marx.

usual, being a critique of post-Hegelian thinking in their homeland. They wrote it, they said, "to settle accounts with our
former philosophic conscience."

It is a ferocious, vindictive, angry work, at times turgid and
obtuse. The Germans are, to select one of many abusive terms
they employed, "cretins" and are accused of having turned
philosophy into an industry.

> When the German market was glutted, and the commodity in
> spite of all efforts found no response in the world-market, the
> business was spoiled in the usual German manner by fake and
> shoddy production, deterioration in quality, adulteration of the
> raw materials, falsification of labels, fake purchases, bill-jobbing
> and a credit system devoid of any real basis.

Marx and Engels state about the Germans, "First of all, an
abstraction is made from a fact; then it is declared that the fact
is based upon an abstraction," though they themselves were not
free from such a charge. Yet, invective aside, the work contains
much of interest and of importance, ideas which they were later
to absorb and develop in other works. They restate the dialectic
of history—one force struggling with another to form a third,
which again struggles with a new challenger. They see two
aspects to human activity: the first, peoples' relationship with
nature and their influence on it, which they call production; and
second, social communication, that is, peoples' relationship
with each other, principally in the process of production. The
two, production and social communication, are interdependent,
but production is the definitive factor. Historically, human beings "begin to distinguish themselves from animals as soon as
they begin to *produce* the necessary means of subsistence."
Finally a dialectic develops: "All collisions in history have their
origin, according to our view, in the contradictions between the

productive forces and the forms of social-communication." In the end, in the materialistic view of history Marx and Engels proclaimed, the proletarian communist revolution is historically necessary and inevitable. "Communism is . . . not merely an ideal to which reality will have to adjust itself but the real movement which abolishes the present state of things." The idea of the dictatorship by the proletariat was first postulated in this sentence:

> Every class which is struggling for mastery, even when its domination, as is the case with the proletariat, postulates the abolition of the old form of society in its entirety and of domination itself, must first conquer for itself political power.

Engels stated later that "the proletarian class will first have to possess itself of the organized political force of the State and with this aid stamp out the resistance of the Capitalist class and reorganize society." Violent revolution, they said in *The German Ideology,* is "necessary . . . not only because the *ruling* class cannot be overthrown in any other way, but also because the class *overthrowing* it can only in a revolution succeed in ridding itself of all the muck of ages and become fit to found society anew."

The world of working-class rule would be a society without private ownership of the means of production, property being under the control of society, the proletariat, as a whole. There would be no divisions into classes as such, no division of labor along class lines, no antithesis between city and country, between mental and physical labor. People would not be alienated from their work. Labor would be a truly free activity of free people, working without compulsion. And people would work in joint efforts, regulating production and developing society according to a general plan. *The German Ideology* was truly a revolutionary work, but Marx's own words describe its fate.

> The manuscript, two big octavo volumes, was already in the hands of a Westphalian publisher when we were informed that altered circumstances rendered publication impossible, whereupon we abandoned our manuscript to the gnawing criticism of the mice. We did so with little regret because our main object had been achieved—we had come to an understanding with ourselves.

The German Ideology, abandoned "to the gnawing criticism of the mice," a phrase that was to become famous, was not published in full until 1932 in the Soviet Union. However, the conclusions Marx and Engels had drawn were to be restated in their succeeding works, *The Poverty of Philosophy* and the shattering pamphlet, *The Communist Manifesto,* which followed shortly afterwards.

3

The First Purges

In 1845 Engels and Marx had made a brief trip to England, staying in London and Manchester for about six weeks. The primary purpose was to study English writings, mainly economic, which were not available on the continent. However, they came into contact with the London office of a group of emigrant and German workers, who were soon to play a decisive role in their lives. In fact, if Engels and Marx had not met these men, communism would today lack one of its most crucial documents, *The Communist Manifesto*. The émigrés had set up an office for their organization, which was known as the League of the Just.

The League had been founded almost ten years previously, as a splinter organization of a group known as the Federation of Exiles, a secret organization founded in Paris in 1834 to work against the Prussian state. The Federation had clandestine cells in a number of German cities. In 1836 a group of dissenters, who wanted more emphasis on social questions, broke away and founded the League of the Just, setting up dual headquarters in Paris and London. The London office was run by three artisans, Joseph Moll, a watchmaker, Karl Schapper, a former student who had become a typesetter, and Heinrich Bauer, a shoemaker. The French historian Jean Sigman has remarked that the leaders of the League "belonged to those trades which provided opportunities for reflection or day-dreams [while working] and thus supplied the workers' movement with so many militants at its beginning." Moll, Schapper, and Bauer were more impressed by Marx and Engels than they were with the workers; the League wanted both of them to join, while Marx and Engels were content to keep the relationship merely confined to correspondence.

While Marx was involved in *The German Ideology,* his living conditions became worse and worse. Jenny Marx said, "My time is always meanly divided between big and small worries and all the cares and troubles of daily life." With his increasing poverty and daily difficulties, Marx became more and more intransigent and dogmatic about his own righteousness. Desperate as his finances were, he would choose righteousness over his own survival. When a group of German socialists raised a substantial sum of money for him, he returned it to them because he was about to attack that very group. Even when the socialists tried to make it clear that the money was a personal, not a political, matter and he should see that the two were separate, he still refused.

He maintained a tremendous pride as a revolutionary who would surrender to no one. The Russian liberal writer, Pavel Annenkov, who visited Marx during this period described his dictatorial manner.

> He was typical of the kind of man who is made up of energy, willpower and unshakable conviction, a type that is highly remarkable even at first glance. With a thick black mane of hair on his head, his hands covered with hairs, his coat buttoned up awry, he nevertheless gave the appearance of a man who has the right and the power to command attention, however odd his appearance and his actions might seem. His movements were awkward, but bold and self-confident; his manners ran positively counter to all the usual social conventions. But they were proud, with a trace of contempt, and his harsh voice which rang like metal was curiously in keeping with the radical judgments on men and things that he let fall. He always spoke in imperative phrases that would brook no resistance; moreover his words were sharpened by what seemed to me an almost painful tone which rang through everything he said. This tone expressed a firm conviction that it was his mission to dominate other minds and prescribe laws for them. I was faced with the incarnation of a democratic dictator, such as one's imagination might have created.

Yet this "dictator" of Annenkov's was hardly "democratic," for Marx saw all about him men who threatened the tiny communist movement he was now fashioning. He had gathered about him a hard core of radicals who would be the leaders of the coming revolution. This group was labeled the Brussels Communist Correspondence Committee, and its function was to work out revolutionary techniques and to bring together all

the communists of Europe into one central network. The task
of establishing this movement was a tremendous one, for in
many countries the workers were not united, and many of them
were illiterate or beyond the easy reach of Communist propaganda. Marx had a core group of eighteen men, including Engels, a man named Wilhelm Wolff, who was to play an
important role in his later life, and various other intellectuals
and artisans. The most important member of the artisan group
was a journeyman tailor, Wilhelm Weitling, who was one of the
few true proletarians in the movement and at thirty-seven by
far the oldest.

Weitling was born the illegitimate son of a laundress and an
unknown French officer during Napoleon's occupation of the
Rhineland, and he had grown up in abysmal poverty. As a child
he had been apprenticed to a tailor, and after he had been forced
into military service, he deserted and became a wandering
preacher of revolutionary ideas.

One's view of Weitling depends on what sources one follows
and where one stands politically. To the early communists he
was a folk hero; to orthodox Marxists, after their original en-
thusiasm, he was undisciplined, egocentric, and vain. Marx had
called him "the German Cinderella" for his original understanding of the revolution that was to come. Weitling had said
it was inevitable, adding "all existing things carry within themselves the seed and the nutriment of revolution." Weitling was
self-taught, an earnest and fearless visionary, and an eloquent
speaker and leader in the tradition of the peasant heroes of the
uprisings of the Middle Ages. There were men like him, artisans
and peasants, scattered about Europe.

At the age of thirty, Weitling had joined a radical uprising
in Paris led by Louis-Auguste Blanqui. After the revolt failed,
Weitling found refuge in Switzerland, only to be arrested for a

mystical revolutionary pamphlet called *The Gospel of a Poor Sinner,* which the authorities found blasphemous (he had called Christ both a communist and an illegitimate child). Weitling spent three months in prison and then continued his wanderings, by now suffering from well-founded delusions of persecution, which turned him into something of a crank. But he was a communist saint too, for he lived in ascetic simplicity, owning nothing but the tools of his trade. In London he was taken up by the Chartists; everywhere he was a hero, for his experiences and his teachings touched the hearts of his hearers. His *Guarantees of Harmony and Freedom* was highly praised by Marx and became one of his revolutionary sources. Weitling preached a class war of the poor against the rich. Sheer terrorism was advocated as one of the means of winning the revolution, the battles to be fought by the "lumpen proletariat," a term he used to describe the most abandoned and desperate elements of society, the hardened criminals and outlaws, who, by the sheer desperation of their lives, would fight to avenge themselves on the oppressors. Weitling saw them as the shock troops, for he believed that the workers would fight only so far, until they achieved their immediate goals and would not carry the battle through until the end.

Weitling had no understanding of the dialectic of history nor of the European philosophers. He worked by instinct. Because he was ignorant of the laws Marx had "discovered," of the dialectic between feudalism and the rising bourgeoisie, between the bourgeoisie and the newly developing proletariat, Weitling viewed the communist revolution as necessarily arising in a spontaneous outbreak. Therefore, having clearly taken a position contrary to Marx's, he was to be purged. Engels remarked later of Weitling that:

He was no longer the naive young journeyman tailor . . . but now the great man, persecuted by the envious on account of his superiority, who scented rivals, secret enemies, and traps everywhere—the prophet, driven from country to country, who carried a recipe for the realization of heaven on earth ready-made in his pocket, and who was possessed by the idea that everyone intended to steal it from him.

Ironically, the description might have fitted Marx as well.

Marx called a meeting of the Committee which had the secret purpose of getting rid of Weitling. The meeting was packed with Marx's own supporters, and Engels led the attack against the journeyman tailor, accusing him of not cooperating with the group. Annenkov, who was present, wrote that Engels stood "tall and erect and as dignified and as serious as an Englishman," while Marx sat at the other end of the table "pencil in hand and his leonine head bent over a sheet of paper." Thus, Weitling was flanked by his two chief opponents, and their supporters were all about him. He was completely surprised by the attack, and for a few moments he fumbled about for words as the torrent of abuse continued. Then he gained his composure, and made the point that he was one of the few proletarians in the party of the proletariat, while Marx gained his knowledge of the workers by his studies, and that he did not feel he should submit himself to the rule of men who had evolved theories far removed from the practical struggles of the ordinary worker.

But under the circumstances, it was a futile speech and Weitling was voted out of the inner circle. He was, however, allowed to sit in on the "trial" of another man, Hermann Kriege, who had emigrated to America and founded a radical paper in New York which advocated not only communism but "universal love," an idea that disgusted Marx. Kriege also campaigned for a law to stop the sale of land to the rich and to give it free to workers. Marx drew up a manifesto against Kriege, denouncing him as a defector, saying, "Kriege's childish methods are in the highest degree compromising to the Communist party in Europe and America." Marx particularly disliked Kriege's land reform program, for he himself in the manifesto against Kriege, laid down a practice which was to be carried out in Russia, China, and other Communist countries in the future, which was that while the Communists could promise land to the peasants *before* the revolution, afterwards they would take it for the state. A second printed attack followed, and Kriege saw his followers slipping away. His paper soon failed, and Kriege is now recalled primarily as an early victim of a Marxist purge.

But this was only the beginning of the struggle to purify the party of dissident elements. A man named Karl Grün, who had been a fellow student with Marx at Berlin, was next on the list. Grün had joined the attack on Weitling, but that did not prove his orthodoxy. One of Grün's sins was failing to realize that, in Marx's view, the development of capitalism was a necessary part of the dialectic. Grün believed that Germany could leap over the capitalistic stage of history into the "Communist paradise." Engels promptly made the rounds of Grün's friends and denounced Grün and Moses Hess, who was now on Marx's enemy list also. Both believed in a moral approach to the development of the perfect society and felt that force, no matter for what purpose, defeated its own end because it brutalized both bourgeoisie and proletariat and made them unable to enjoy true freedom. They also said that industrialization was a grave danger, that the revolution must be achieved by peaceful means before the machine became dominant, otherwise the result would be a bloody class war. Grün and Hess stated that by making the proletariat the ruling class, Marx was only enslaving the other elements of society. The ideal state was one in which all people were free, not the workers alone.

But to Marx this was a program bordering on the point of idiocy because it depended on the good will of the people in power, and he did not believe that they would be willing to relinquish the powers they had acquired by birth, ability, or wealth.

The next victim on Marx's list was Hess, "the Communist rabbi," as Engels sarcastically called him. Hess had defended Weitling, and he was a friend of Grün. He was a man of great education, experience, sophistication, and shrewdness, who saw the course of events dictated by Marx's drive for power. Rather than become enmeshed in a hopeless fight in which abuse and invective were employed in preference to rational argument, he decided to resign from the party. Nevertheless, he was to remain active in radical causes.

In his attack on Grün, Marx had tried to enlist the help of the French socialist Pierre Joseph Proudhon. Previously Marx had been an admirer of Proudhon, for like Weitling he came of peasant background, was eloquent and intelligent in his analysis of the problems facing the working classes, and was an excellent writer. Proudhon's famous work is *What Is Property?*, published in 1840, in which he argued that "property is theft," a phrase that touched the heart of the tenant farmer, who spent his life working on other people's land, and the artisans, who could never hope to own even a small piece of it.

Proudhon favored the abolition of large holdings of land and its distribution among the peasants and workers. He also condemned capitalistic profit making and exploitation and usury. Marx admitted Proudhon's heartfelt "indignation at the infamy of what exists" and his "strong muscular style as a writer."

Like other events in Marx's life, what happened next is open to dispute. The official Marxist-Leninist version is that Marx "hoped Proudhon would overcome the defects of his outlook [and] sought to help Proudhon broaden his outlook and understand Hegel's dialectics." However, "Proudhon practically refused to collaborate, and took a negative attitude," saying Marx's proposals were an invitation to "gross arbitrary acts, violence and annihilation." What Marx had actually asked Proudhon to do was to join a secret revolutionary society which would be prepared for "the moment of action." In the postscript to the letter in which he proposed this terrorist group, he denounced Grün as "a charlatan and a parasite," who "conceals his ignorance in pompous phrases and arrogant sentences," and "abuses the friendships he had formed with well-known authors in order to elevate himself and compromise them."

Proudhon replied that he could not go along with the torture or abuse of property holders because he felt that making them martyrs would gain them the sympathy of the public.

At this point, Marx saw Proudhon not as an ally to be brought into the coming revolutionary struggle but as an enemy to be destroyed as fiercely as the bourgeoisie would be destroyed at some future time. He now began an attack on Proudhon as crude and as vicious as upon any other of his enemies. Many of Proudhon's ideas were widely popular throughout Europe, and a number of them survived, being absorbed into what was later known as syndicalism, a form of anarchism popular among workers and peasants in France, Italy, and Spain. Though Proudhon lacked the depth of Marx's education, he was still a capable social thinker. By profession a typesetter, he was thus a member of the artisan class. His peasant background had installed a certain narrowness and puritanism in him; otherwise he was fearless and possessed great moral strength. In fact, it was Proudhon's insistence on viewing the problems of the proletariat in terms of morality as well as politics that infuriated Marx. Proudhon saw the state as an instrument in the hands of a small minority being used to rob the majority of the people. He believed that a "mutualist" cooperative system was the answer, for competition brutalizes people, and the accumulation of capital enables the rich to dominate the mass of the people. He said, also, that it was useless to try to convert the rich to cooperation with the people, for their altruistic instincts had long ago withered away. And he thought that political organization by the workers would in turn lead to a new form of tyranny. What he saw, after the stolen property had been returned to the rightful owners, was that each man would have a minimum piece of land in order to maintain his personal independence and his moral and social dignity.

There was nothing here that Marx could appreciate. Proudhon made the error of thinking that, though they had some disagreements, he and Marx could still carry on a discussion in a civilized manner, and he let Marx see the manuscript of a new work, *The Philosophy of Poverty.* To Marx it was full of "errors," and he saw no choice but to destroy the author and his work. His answer was a ponderous work, sparked with some witticism at the expense of his rival, entitled *The Poverty of Philosophy*, a bitter attack in which he denounced Proudhon as "the philosopher and economist of the middle class." Proudhon claimed that Marx had misstated his ideas, attributed thoughts he had never entertained, and, in short, had falsified the concepts laid out in the original. To non-Communists, Marx's attack is heavy handed, often dull, and it is seldom read. The Communists saw it differently. Engels said it described "our program," and Lenin considered it one of the first truly mature Marxist works. At any rate, the attack helped sharpen Marx's own views and strengthen his belief in the coming struggle for power. Where Proudhon had asked for a peaceful development of a new society, Marx saw that class antagonisms were bound to result in acute social conflict. A working-class victory would mean that "*social evolutions* will cease to be *political* revolutions." Marx concludes *The Poverty of Philosophy* with a quotation from the French writer George Sand: "Combat or death, bloody struggle or extinction. It is thus that the question is inexorably put."

A few years later Moses Hess, looking back upon the purges and especially his own defeat at the hands of Marx, wrote, "It is a terrible pity that this man, who is easily the most gifted member of our Party, is too proud to be content with all the recognition he has earned from those who know and value his achievements; it is a pity he seems to demand a kind of personal submission which I for one will never concede to any man."

Thus, with the party cleansed of heretical elements, Marx felt secure in his role as leader, prophet, and philosopher.

4

The Call to the Workers of the World

What Marx had accomplished thus far was to lay the ground plan for his life and that of the revolution. He saw himself as preeminent of all revolutionaries: only *his* theories were true, all others being suspect. His predecessors and contemporaries, no matter how great they may have stood in the world, were all worthless, false, contemptible, even ludicrous. Some he actually considered speakers for a petty bourgeois point of view. Even workers like Weitling or those of peasant background like Proudhon were tainted with bourgeois ideology. Only Marx and his collaborator Engels could preach the true, purified revolution. There was no wisdom except Marx's, no gospel but Marx's, no science but as it was interpreted by Marx. So there he stood, the self-proclaimed leader of the revolution. What was to be the next step?

What happened at this point was one of those turns of fate which is in part coincidence, in part determined by historical events, and in part determined by the ability to seize the moment and turn it to one's own advantage. The League of the Just in London had changed its name to the Communist League in the summer of 1847. Its principles were vague, which was one reason Marx and Engels had not wanted to join the group, and now its leaders were trying to formulate some kind of coherent program of their aims. The League was committed to social change, and that change was to be effected by violence. Moll, Schapper, and Bauer, who were the core of the League, wanted some kind of written "catechism" which would explain their plans. Schapper had tried a version but lacked the necessary literary skill. He called upon Moses Hess, who was then in Paris, for help. Hess produced a draft, which he sent to Engels for an opinion. But Engels did a scurrilous thing. He scrapped Hess's draft and wrote his own. He told Marx about his act, saying, "*Just between ourselves,* I played a hellish trick on Mosi." Hess had no idea that his work had been betrayed. The Engels version was sent to the League lenders in London, who believed that Hess had written it. "We shall have it all our way," wrote Engels to Marx, adding, "Even the devil must not know about it, otherwise we shall be deposed and there will be a murderous scandal."

The Engels catechism was called *A Confession of Faith* and was structured upon eighteen questions asked by a naive but eager seeker of the revolutionary truth of a Wise Old Communist. In simple terms it tried to outline the more complex and ponderous doctrines that Marx and Engels had evolved over the last few years, especially the doctrine of the proletariat as the new base for society, its antithesis to the bourgeoisie, the laws of social development, the seizure of power and of private property by the workers, and the replacement of the state by a workers' state. Engels was not satisfied with this version and wrote a second, which ran about four times the length of the original. It was now called *Principles of Communism.* But he still was not satisfied with the results. At the end of November of the same year, Engels and Marx traveled to London for a meeting with the leaders of the Communist League, who still believed that the text of their catechism had been done by Hess upon Schapper's draft.

Marx and Engels now saw that they had a chance to take over the League by the force of their will. They constantly denigrated the other men, who though shrewd artisans and able to get along with their fellow workers, were not skilled in political invective and parliamentary tactics. Marx demanded the task of producing a final version of the catechism. Moll, Schapper, and Bauer resisted for ten days of stormy maneuvering but finally surrendered, and Marx and Engels returned to their homes, Marx to Brussels and Engels to Paris. After Engels had received various drafts through the mails, he wrote Marx, "I believe we had better drop the catechism form and call the thing Communist *Manifesto.*" Marx worked through December and into January. The three leaders of the League, Moll, Schapper, and Bauer, had become impatient with Marx's apparent delays; they had not wanted more than a short and simple document. On January 26th, 1848, they wrote to Marx and gave him an ultimatum to finish the work by the first of February or, "Further measures will be taken against you."

They also demanded the return of all their documents if he did not complete the job on time. Marx had the manuscript in the mail a few days later, and indeed the last two chapters show signs of being done quickly. The work, written in German, was quickly set in type by a print shop run by German Communist émigrés in London. The title was *Manifest der Kommunistischen Partei,* or as we know it, *The Communist Manifesto.* The little book was elegantly designed and well printed and its appearance led to the remark that it looked like a book of love poems.

The first copies were ready for shipment to the continent in the beginning of March. A month later it went into a second printing, and translations were made into other languages (four in French alone). Engels immediately translated it into English, but this version did not appear for another two years. By the end of 1848 *The Communist Manifesto* had appeared in French, Spanish, Danish, Polish, Italian, and Swedish; it was eventually translated into all of the European languages in the next decades and probably has seen as many translations as the Bible. The current "official" English version was translated by Samuel Moore in 1888 from the original German and edited and annotated by Engels. The prose is clear, sinewy, and graphic. When the authentic English edition appeared, Engels remarked that the *Manifesto* was "the most popular, the most international work of all socialist literature, the common platform accepted by millions of workingmen from Siberia to California." And what does this notorious document say, this slight pamphlet printed originally in a language which could be understood by few except the handful of émigrés and exiles?

It opens with the striking phrase which even communism's enemies know: "A spectre is haunting Europe—the spectre of Communism."

The word "spectre" is strange, yet it is the word selected by Engels and Moore in their translations. The Concise Oxford Dictionary defines it as "Ghost; haunting presentiment (*of* ruin, war, madness, &c.)." It comes from the Latin spectrum, which means an "image of something seen continuing when the eyes are closed or turned away."

Thus this Communist spectre is haunting, will haunt Europe, though "all the Powers of old Europe have entered into a holy alliance to exorcise this spectre: Pope and Czar, Metternich and Guizot, French Radicals and German police spies."

Two facts are obvious according to the pamphlet.

I. Communism is already acknowledged by all European Powers to be itself a Power.

II. It is high time that Communists should openly, in the face of the whole world, publish their views, their aims, their tendencies, and meet this nursery tale of the Spectre of Communism with a Manifesto of the party itself.

Marx and Engels then proceed to an outline, admirably concise and admirably clear, of the situation.

The history of all hitherto existing society is the history of class struggles.

Freeman and slave, patrician and plebeian, lord and serf, guildmaster and journeyman, in a word, oppressor and oppressed, stood in constant opposition to one another, carried on an uninterrupted, now hidden, now open fight, a fight that each time ended, either in a revolutionary re-constitution of society at large, or in the common ruin of the contending classes.

This battle is given a few paragraphs, and then the authors say that in the present epoch, that of the bourgeoisie, it has been simplified because now there are only two classes directly facing each other: bourgeoisie and proletariat.

Tracing the growth of the bourgeoisie from the serfs of the Middle Ages to the discovery of the colonial world, which opened up new markets and new sources of raw materials while the old feudal order was dying out, they state that an entirely new system took over.

> Steam and machinery revolutionized industrial production. The place of manufacture [handwork and handcrafts] was taken by the giant, modern industry, the place of the industrial middle class, by industrial millionaires, the leaders of whole industrial armies, the modern bourgeois. . . . The bourgeoisie, historically, has played a most revolutionary part.

The bourgeoisie, state Marx and Engels, in one of the crucial and blunt passages of the Manifesto, have pitilessly destroyed "all feudal, patriarchal, idyllic relations" that bound men to each other in the past and have "left remaining no other nexus between man and man than naked self-interest, than callous 'cash' payment." For all other forms of exploitation of the past, "it has substituted naked, shameless, direct, brutal exploitation." Even the family relation is now but "a mere money relation."

In the past conservation of old modes of production in unaltered form was "the first condition of existence for all earlier industrial classes. But today "constant revolutionizing of production . . . everlasting uncertainty and agitation distinguish the bourgeois epoch from all earlier ones." Now "man is at last compelled to face with sober senses, his real conditions of life and his relations with his kind."

The bourgeoisie, "through its exploitation of the world market [has] given a cosmopolitan character to production and consumption in every country," and "raw material [is] drawn from the remotest zones; industries whose products are consumed, not only at home, but in every quarter of the globe [destroy] old local and national self sufficiency." The result is that cheap prices destroy the old ways of living, for all nations, on pain of extinction, are forced to imitate the bourgeois method of both production and of living.

This damning indictment of the bourgeois industrial world, though written a century and a half ago, treats of planned obsolescence and international conglomerates with insight and dire warnings. Engels, forty-five years later, was to add the observation that "step by step, the small and middle landowner-ship of the farmers [in America], the basis of the whole political constitution, is succumbing to the competition of giant farms." This is what is sometimes called agribusiness today, the great corporate farm holdings which increase steadily, while the small family farm dies out. Engels also added that in America "simultaneously, a mass proletariat and a fabulous concentration of capitals are developing for the first time in the industrial regions."

On the question of the abolition of private property, Marx and Engels took different views at different times in their lives, the issue is still a point of contention among even the most orthodox Marxists. But the Manifesto states bluntly: "You reproach us with intending to do away with your property. Precisely so; that is just what we intend." However, this harsh step has been qualified, for they have said in a previous passage, "The distinguishing feature of Communism is not the abolition of property generally, but the abolition of bourgeois property." They ask, how can the "hard-won, self-acquired, self-earned property," the property of the petty artisan and the small farmer, be abolished when much of it has already been taken

by the bourgeois industrialists, who add to their holdings daily.
The bourgeois family is another target.

> The bourgeois clap-trap about the family and education [which
> has been perverted for bourgeois propaganda purposes], about
> the hallowed co-relation of parent and child, becomes all the
> more disgusting, the more, by the action of Modern Industry,
> all family ties among the proletarians are torn asunder, and their
> children transformed into simple articles of commerce and in-
> struments of labor.

"The bourgeois sees in his wife a mere instrument of production," and he fears that under communism, women, like machines, will be communalized. But:

> The Communists have no need to introduce community of
> women; it has existed almost from time immemorial. Our bour-
> geois, not content with having the wives and daughters of their
> proletarians at their disposal, not to speak of common prosti-
> tutes, take the greatest pleasure in seducing each other's
> wives. Bourgeois marriage is in reality a system of wives in
> common. . . .

After abolishing a number of other bourgeois institutions,
such as national boundaries, religion, and morality, the Manifesto comes to grips with the central program of communism.
It must be noted, however, that this program was essentially a
stripping away of the chains that bound the proletariat (the
workman, Marx and Engels had said, is only "an appendage of
the machine"). But from this freeing and cleansing will come
true freedom, "a most radical rupture with traditional property
relations," the worker—man, woman, or child—being no more
than another form of property. The workers will have to attack
both bourgeois property and bourgeois production.

There is no clear description of the future state resulting from this "revolutionizing," but the following ten points are laid down. I quote them in full, for many of them have already been achieved, not only in the Marxist nations but in capitalistic countries as well. Marxists would say that non-Communist countries granted these points not because of conviction but merely as a series of concessions to control the proletariat.

1. Abolition of property in land and application of all rents of land to public purposes.

2. A heavy progressive or graduated income tax.

3. Abolition of all rights of inheritance.

4. Confiscation of the property of all emigrants and rebels.

5. Centralization of credit in the hands of the State, by means of a national bank with State capital and an exclusive monopoly.

6. Centralization of the means of communication and transport in the hands of the State.

7. Extension of factories and instruments of production owned by the State; the bringing into cultivation of waste lands, and the improvement of the soil generally in accordance with a common plan.

8. Equal liability of all to labor. Establishment of industrial armies, especially for agriculture.

9. Combination of agriculture with manufacturing industries; gradual abolition of the distinction between town and country, by a more equable distribution of the population over the country.

10. Free education for all children in public schools. Abolition of children's factory labor in its present form. Combination of education with industrial production, &c., &c.

The Manifesto states that by the accomplishment of at least these basic points, the proletariat will "have swept away the conditions for the existence of class antagonisms and of classes generally, and will thereby have abolished its own supremacy as a class. In place of the old bourgeois society, with its classes and class antagonism, we shall have an association, in which the free development of each is the condition for the free development of all."

The third section of the Manifesto attacks the various other socialist, communist, and utopian "do-good" movements, which Marx saw as such a threat to himself and his form of communism. Most of them, with the exception of what is now called anarcho-syndicalism, have disappeared into history.

The final section of the Manifesto, a short one, concludes with a list of the groups or parties in other countries with whom the Communists will work (at least for the present), and here Marx sees his homeland as the key power, for Germany "is on the eve of a bourgeois revolution . . . which will be but the prelude to an immediately following proletarian revolution."

The Manifesto concludes with this paragraph:

> The Communists disdain to conceal their views and aims. They openly declare that their ends can be attained only by the forcible overthrow of all existing social conditions. Let the ruling classes tremble at a Communist revolution. The proletarians have nothing to lose but their chains. They have a world to win.

WORKING MEN OF ALL COUNTRIES, UNITE!

Such is the official English translation with which the Manifesto concludes. The German has been more euphoniously translated, "Workers of the world, unite!" followed by, "You have nothing to lose but your chains." However translated, the phrase was already used by Schapper as the slogan for a periodical named *Kommunistiche Zeitung,* which had appeared in September, 1847. (Only a single issue appeared.) The Manifesto was to spend over two decades in limbo, for very little attention was paid to it until after the Paris Commune of 1871, when workers all over the world began to read it. Despite the most fervent expectations of both Marx and Engels, the Manifesto had no effect upon the uprisings of 1848 and 1849. Today, it stands as a seminal work of Communist literature.

And as for those catalytic agents, Josef Moll lost his life in southern Germany during the revolts of 1849. Heinrich Bauer emigrated to Australia in 1851, and Karl Schapper, after a period of estrangement with Marx and Engels, remained a member of the central committee of the First International.

5

The Final Exile

While the Manifesto was being printed, a totally unrelated event shook the continent, though later the Communists were to try to take some credit for it. Groups of moderates, liberals, and radicals—including some socialists—in Paris had reached the point under the aging King Louis Philippe, the Bankers' King, that they began to meet and demonstrate in protest. The people took to the streets on February 22, 1848, and set up barricades. Troops were ordered out, among them the National Guard. To the surprise of the government, eleven of the twelve contingents of the guard showed strong support for their fellow workers and shopkeepers in the streets. On February 24, a most unfortunate event happened, which was to energize the lower classes to overthrow the government. A group of some two hundred clashed with a detachment of troops in the center of the city. A shot rang out—no one knows who fired it—and the troops emptied their rifles into the demonstrators. When the fusillade was over, seventeen people, including two women, lay dead on the cobblestone pavement, and fifty were wounded. Now the demonstration had turned into a funeral cortège. Carrying the bodies of the victims, the workers slowly marched into the dank alleyways of the slums, lighting their way by torches.

The workers now turned into rebels. Tens of thousands took up posts behind barricades. City life was at a standstill, and the government was paralyzed. The ten thousand troops ordered to attack the workers were demoralized, and most of the National Guard appeared to be going over to the rebels. The troops surrendered and were disarmed. King Louis Philippe decided to abdicate, turning the crown over to his ten-year-old nephew. To put some semblance of order into the collapsing scene, seven leading citizens, moderates and bourgeois, assumed control, presumably on behalf of the people. But shortly afterwards four radical journalists, among them a newspaper editor whom Marx included as one of his allies, forced themselves into the group and announced that they too were part of the new government. The eleven ministers of the citizenry stood on the balcony of the Paris city hall to the acclaim of the crowd. It was "the will of the people," the revolutionaries told the rest of France in asserting the authority of the new government over the entire nation. All of this had happened by February 25.

The news swept Europe, and within days, weeks at the most, virtually all of the continent was in revolt, either against foreign rule (as the Italians against the Austrians; the Poles against Germans, Austrians, and Russians or their own rulers; the Germans against other Germans; the Viennese against the notorious Metternich, the prime minister of the Hapsburgs). Most of the German cities of the Rhineland were taken over by democratic movements, and soon the uprisings reached Berlin itself.

Marx, in Brussels, did not have long to wait before being involved, though in a minor way, with the French workers. On March 3, the Belgian government, having seen copies of the Manifesto and being understandably nervous about this man who had violated his promise not to write anything political, ordered Marx to leave. The police had visited him at five in the afternoon; he was given twenty-four hours in which to get ready. Marx called together five members of the Communist League who had been visiting him with the express purpose of shifting the league's headquarters from London to Paris, and told them of his expulsion. The decision was made to liquidate the Belgian office and to move everything to Paris. The men left, and the police returned and arrested Marx. He and his wife had hoped to be able to get their belongings together, but Marx spent the next twenty-four hours in a jail cell, and since he had not left during that period, as the government had ordered, he was summarily expelled without a chance to get papers or clothes. The next day Marx and his family arrived in Paris, where with other exiles, he set up anew the Central Committee of the Communist League.

In the midst of the Parisian revolution, the German émigrés were concerned about their own country. Riots had already broken out among the peasants in southwest Germany, and in a few days open revolts began to develop throughout Germany. Other émigré groups were in the process of forming armed legions to help the liberation of their own people. While the Poles, Belgians, Irish, Spaniards, and Italians were already on their way to fight, Marx flatly rejected any armed intervention by German Communists, though most of the other members of the league had voted for it. Marx stated that the best members of the league would be arrested and killed as they crossed the borders into their homeland. Engels, who went off on his own anyway, said later:

> We opposed this playing with revolution in the most decisive fashion. To carry an invasion, which was to import the revolution forcibly from outside, into the midst of the ferment then going on in Germany, meant to undermine the revolution in

Engels often cartooned the Emperor and his liberal bourgeoisie. He and Marx thought both would soon be overthrown by the proletariat in a series of democratic revolutions.

Germany itself, to strengthen the government and to deliver the legionaires defenceless into the hands of the German troops.

They solved the problem for the moment, not by action in the field against the government, but by drawing up a program (outlined in a broadside), "Demands of the Communist Party in Germany," which called for a unified nation, "a single indivisible republic." Estates, mines, collieries, public transport, and banks were to be nationalized. The expectation was that the bourgeois revolution would be followed by a proletarian revolution. But neither happened at that time. And then, believing that the current uprisings in Germany were bound to fail, they sent their would-be troops to Germany not to fight but rather to organize offices of the Communist League. Marx himself, with his family, went to Cologne early in April to prepare for the founding of a new newspaper, to be called the *Neue Rheinische Zeitung.* He had trouble raising capital, because he had to ask money of the very bourgeois businessmen that he was about to denounce. He was able to scrape together enough funds to begin publishing by June. The paper was unabashedly Communist, with its primary contributors the members of the Communist League.

Marx guided the paper with an iron hand, and his contributors wrote according to his wishes, not their own. Engels remarked afterwards that the constitution of the paper allowed "simply dictatorship by Marx." Nevertheless, in the fifty-five weeks of its publication (a total of 301 issues), it was a highly professional journal, and the best of the Communist and socialist press ever to appear.

Meanwhile the revolutionary forces across Europe were running into hard times. The Parisian rebels failed to gain the

In 1848 workers and revolutionaries across Europe arose against the old order. This is street fighting in Paris.

support of the French peasants, and by the end of June, the workers having suffered some disastrous defeats at the hands of the regular army brought in from the provinces, the uprising was finished. In December of the same year Louis Napoleon, the nephew of the late emperor, was elected president by a wide margin over his left-wing opponents in a vote brought about ironically by the workers, who had demanded universal suffrage. In this case the conservative peasants, voting for the first time, put in office the man the workers hated.

Marx could take a long, historical view of the tragedy of the French proletariat, for it was the working out of the dialectic of history. He expressed the opinion that the survivors of those who had been killed by the workers would be looked after by the state, who would honor those fallen as "protectors of order." On the other hand,

> The common people are torn by hunger, reviled by the press, abandoned by the doctors, abused by honest folk as thieves, incendiaries, and galley-slaves; their wives and children are plunged into even deeper misery, and their finest spirits are deported overseas. To bind the laurel round their grim brows, that is the privilege, indeed the right of the democratic press.

He added: "They have been defeated but their enemies are vanquished."

Marx had a gloomy, volcanic hatred for Russia and Russians and indeed virtually all Slavic people. This now became one of his causes. Mikhail Bakunin had called for Slavic unity against oppressive rule. Marx denounced this as "so-called democratic Pan-Slavism," and said, "All Pan-Slavists set nationality, that is to say, imaginary universal-Slav nationality—before revolution." Engels added, "For Germans, hatred of Russia must always be the primary revolutionary quality. . . . Mere phrases and plans for a vague democratic future in these countries are not going to prevent us from treating our enemies as enemies." Marx summed up their enmity by stating:

> War with Russia is the only war for revolutionary Germany; this is the only war that will cleanse the misdeeds of the past, the only war in which we can take heart and defeat our own autocrats. In this war, as befits a nation shaking off the chains of a long and indolent slavery, Germany can purchase the spread of civilization by sacrificing her sons, and make herself free by gaining freedom without.

Not only did Marx oppose the common sentiment of the Communist League and the readers of his paper in refusing to support the German Legion and the concept of Slav nationalism, he also made a radical about-face which left his followers completely confused. The Communists (through the Workers Union) proposed running worker candidates for the Frankfurt Assembly. Marx rejected the idea of such independent candidates and also the program of a working-class revolution proclaimed by the Communists. He instead advocated a coalition between the workers and the liberal bourgeoisie. Marx believed that while the German proletariat was philosophically ready for revolt, politically it was not. Before the workers could take over, the bourgeoisie would have to establish and consolidate their own revolution against the remnants of the feudal and noble classes, and only then could the true revolution of the workers come. It was a basic plank in Marx's platform that, when it would work to their own advantage, the workers would fight alongside the middle classes, though there would always be an intrinsic opposition between the two groups. This was always to be a common Communist practice, beginning with the first successful Marxist revolution in Russia, when the Bolsheviks—the Communists—took over after the moderates, the Mensheviks, had overthrown the Czar.

The alliance between worker and bourgeois was effected solely for the purpose of ousting the oppressive ruling classes that stood above both. Marx believed that the bourgeoisie, who had their own desire to be liberated, were capable of bearing the brunt of the struggle, while the workers, who were ill-educated, uninformed, and still disorganized, were not capable of a successful revolution. Meanwhile, around him, the situation was in a muddle. Some of his followers wanted an immediate revolt of the workers without the aid of the middle classes; others wanted a quick but bloodless revolution. Marx and Engels stood virtually alone in their determination not to let the Communists

From France the 1848 revolution spread to Berlin (above) and other capitals. But Marx and Engels refused support.

become involved before the workers were ready. Marx's fighting was carried on in the pages of the *Neue Rheinische Zeitung.* His investors gradually faded away in the flood of revolutionary rhetoric, and Marx had an open field and free reign to say what he wanted. His material ranged from the deeply analytical to blunt calls for a future "revolutionary terrorism." His writing was often violent, vindictive, and striking. His own acts were decisive. To stem the opposition to his apparent caution, he soon dissolved the Communist League, not with a democratic vote, for he would have been outvoted, but by the power of his fiat. For the year, Marx and the *Neue Rheinische Zeitung* were the party and the workers' movement. The ousted and unaligned groups denounced Marx as "opportunistic," but it was Marx who had the power and the means of expressing it.

His thinking took two major paths, intertwined in his own mind. One was German unity, the other was war with Russia, which Marx regarded as the epitome of reaction and feudalism. Germany, at that time composed of twenty-five different states (of which Prussia was the greatest), was to him weak, inefficient, and politically backward. He had no romantic regard for small nations, and he believed that war with Russia would weld the German principalities into a unified nation. But preach as he might to the bourgeoisie about overthrowing the feudal past, no action resulted. Meanwhile, across Europe, the various entrenched powers began to move against the rebels. Leaders were shot down or imprisoned; the workers and peasants surrendered their arms. In Berlin, Friedrich Wilhelm reasserted his control over Prussia. For the moment Marx lost faith in the ability of the liberal bourgeoisie as well as the masses to advance their own cause. He saw the people as incurably stupid and all too gullible about the promises of the kings and princes, who had no other object in mind but their subjugation. But while the battles were going on throughout Germany, the *Neue Rheinische Zeitung* had its own to handle.

In December, as the result of riots in Cologne, where troops were brought in from outside to restore order, the paper was temporarily suspended. Engels had to flee the city on foot to avoid arrest and escaped to Switzerland. By the end of the year Marx faced charges for a number of seditious articles. In a flurry of independence, the National Assembly at Berlin defied the king and passed a resolution that the people were no longer to pay taxes. Marx wrote, "It is high treason to pay taxes. Refusal to pay taxes is the primary duty of the citizens!" The king ordered the dissolution of the assembly and the closing of the *Neue Rheinische Zeitung.* By this time the staff of the paper had armed themselves, but Marx realized that in case of an assault by the Prussian troops outside, resistance was futile. The last issue of the *Neue Rheinische Zeitung,* printed in red, appeared on May 19, 1849. Marx wrote, in italics, a warning to the king: "We have no compassion, and we ask no compassion from you. When our turn comes, we shall not make excuses for the terror."

With Engels, Marx toured western Germany, visiting left-wing groups, and then, a month after the termination of his paper, he arrived again in Paris. He was completely broke, having used all his money to pay off the staff of the paper and to get to Paris. Jenny Marx followed him a few days later with the children, paying the train fare with the proceeds of the sale of some family silver. Marx turned to Ferdinand Lassalle for a loan. Lassalle started a public collection, infuriating Marx, who said, "I prefer the direst straits to begging." But he was not to remain in Paris either. The new government ordered him expelled from the city, saying he could take up residence in Brittany, which Marx considered unhealthy. He wrote Engels, "You will understand that I shall not agree to this veiled attempt at murder. That is why I am leaving France." His first choice was Switzerland, where most of the people spoke German, but he was denied a visa. He decided upon London, still another place of exile, but one, which it turned out, was to be lifelong. Again he had no money. He left behind Jenny, who was pregnant, and the children and set off for the nation he considered the heart and soul of capitalism, penniless and not knowing a word of the language. He was now thirty-one and still without a career except that of revolutionary.

Jenny and the children soon arrived, and the family took up residence in a small flat in the Chelsea section of London. Here their fourth child, Heinrich Guido, was born on November 5.

From this point on, their living conditions, which had been precarious, degenerated into sheer disaster. Marx's main source of income was his writings, few of which brought much money. He was constantly borrowing from his mother and her relatives and from friends, especially Engels. Borrowing from Henrietta Marx was especially unpleasant because she would urge him to get a job like other people; he was incapable of convincing her that his career as a revolutionary was more important than a lifetime in an office. Loans from no matter whom often turned into gifts because he had no means of repaying them. At times there was absolutely no money at all in the house. The Marxes not only survived on the worst kind of food, and little of it, but Marx could not buy newspapers, writing paper, and stamps nor pay for doctors and medicine. The standard fare was bread and potatoes. At times, for as long as several weeks, Marx could not leave the flat because his coat, trousers, and shoes were in pawn.

By May of the next year Marx was seriously in arrears for the rent and received an eviction notice. "Because we had no money," wrote Jenny Marx to a friend in Germany, "two bailiffs arrived and seized the little I had, beds, linen, dresses, everything, even my poor child's cradle and the girls' best toys as they stood there shedding bitter tears. They threatened to take away everything within two hours. Then I would have lain on the floor with my freezing children and my aching breast." Marx raised some money from friends to settle the rent and got his possessions back, but they were immediately sold off to pay small debts to local tradesmen. The Marxes were forced to move. They found temporary refuge in a German hotel, moved a few days later to another flat, and then in December to a two-room flat in Soho, which was then a terrible slum area and a center for emigrants, mainly from France and Italy. Here the Marxes were to spend six years in destitution. The front room served as a study, living, and dining room, and the rear room as the bedroom for the entire family. By the time the Marxes had found this refuge, tragedy had already struck them, for the new baby had died the previous month.

Engels had now moved to England, going to Manchester where he again took a job in the family firm. At first he was able to send Marx only a small amount of money out of his meager salary, but as he rose in the Engels hierarchy to become a full partner, his contributions to Marx were more substantial. These years of privation did irreparable damage to Marx's health and psyche, and his wife and children were grievously harmed. For years they saw nothing but unending degradation. Marx was psychologically incapable of taking on an ordinary job. Not only would a job have taken him away from the work of the revolution, which he felt was of supreme necessity and importance, but he also lacked the discipline to apply himself to any task other than one which he himself had chosen. He once applied to the British railway system for an office position, but when he presented himself to the hiring office in his frayed clothing and speaking a heavily accented English, he was rejected, and so the diet of bread and potatoes had to continue.

It is against the wretchedness of this existence that he worked out his ideas, proclaimed them as the means, the only means, to the salvation of the working people. Such bareness and poverty must have had a deep effect upon his own thinking, for he was a participant in the very misery of the proletariat that he was describing. The bitterness of Marx's invective, not only against industrialists, landowners, feudal lords and other nobility, the bourgeoisie, and the capitalists, to say nothing of the strange attacks on his co-workers and friends and on others whose ideas he should have respected, must be in part the result of his harsh existence.

He was constantly besieged by creditors. He would send the children downstairs to say, "Mr. Marx hain't home," but the pain of ordinary life could only be spaced out, not eliminated. Unfriendly biographers have called him a bohemian. He was anything but that, and what he wanted above all else was the security of a middle-class existence, with adequate shelter, food, clothing, medical care, and some luxuries.

The misery seemed to be unending. In 1851 he told Engels that Jenny Marx was having hysterical outbreaks and eccentric fits due to their poverty. He feared for her "nervous condition," adding, "At home everything is constantly in a state of siege, streams of tears exasperate me for whole nights at a time and make me completely desperate." But he could add, "I pity my wife. The chief burden falls on her and *au fond* she is right." Unfortunately, Jenny Marx was almost always pregnant. Their daughter Franziska, born in March, 1852, died thirteen months later during one of the family's worst financial crises. Jenny Marx described the sad scene to a woman friend:

> The three children still alive lay beside us, and we wept for the little angel who rested near us, pale and cold. The dear child's death came at the time of our bitterest poverty. I ran into a French refugee who lived nearby and who had visited us shortly beforehand. He showed the greatest sympathy and gave me two pounds. With these we bought the little coffin in which my poor child now slumbers in peace. The child had had no cradle when she came into the world, and this last little dwelling was long denied her.

About the same time Marx wrote to Engels about his problems, saying that for himself he had "complete indifference." But:

> My house is a hospital and the crisis is so disrupting that it requires all my attention. . . . The atmosphere is very dis-

turbed; my wife is ill, Jennychen is ill, and Lenchen has a kind of nervous fever. I couldn't and can't call the doctor, because I have no money for medicine. For eight or ten days I have managed to feed the family on bread and potatoes, but it is still doubtful whether I can get hold of any today. . . . I have written no articles for Dana because I had not a penny to go and read the newspapers. . . . Besides there is the baker, milkman, greengrocer, and old butcher's bills. How can I deal with all this devilish filth?

He added that he had again been forced to borrow a few shillings to keep going. The poverty was squalid, like that of the slum workers Engels had described in the Manchester alleyways, yet there was still a certain style and charm which could surpass even this wretched life of exile. One of the most interesting descriptions of the Marxes at this time comes, strangely, from a Prussian police spy, who posed as an émigré and worked his way into Marx's tiny circle of friends.

He lives in one of the worst and cheapest neighborhoods in London. He occupies two rooms. There is not one clean or decent piece of furniture in either room, everything is broken, tattered and torn, with thick dust over everything . . . manuscripts, books and newspapers lie beside the children's toys, bits and pieces from his wife's sewing basket, cups with broken rims, dirty spoons, knives, forks, lamps, an inkpot, tumblers, pipes, tobacco ash—all piled up on the same table. On entering the room, smoke and tobacco fumes make your eyes water to such an extent that at first you seem to be groping about in a cavern —until you get used to it, and manage to make out certain objects in the haze. Sitting down is a dangerous business. Here is a chair with only three legs, there is another which happens to be whole, on which the children are playing at cooking. That is the one which is offered to the visitor, but the children's cooking is not removed, and if you sit down you risk a pair of trousers. But all these things do not in the least embarrass Marx or his wife. You are received in the most friendly way, and are cordially offered pipes, tobacco, and whatever else there may happen to be. Presently a clever and interesting conversation arises which repays for all the domestic deficiencies and this makes the discomfort bearable.

Meanwhile the children were wasting away—three of Marx's six children were to die of malnutrition and illness. The death that struck Marx the most by all accounts was that of his son Edgar, his favorite child. (He preferred the boys: when Franziska was born he wrote Engels, "My wife has been delivered, unfortunately of a girl and not a boy," and when Eleanor was born in 1855, he wrote again that his wife had again given birth "unfortunately of the 'sex' par excellence. If it had been a male child, the thing would have been better.") Edgar, who was affectionately known as Musch (which means Little Sparrow in German), developed a severe gastric ailment in the spring of 1855, shortly after the birth of Eleanor, the youngest of the girls and the last of Marx's children. In early April he died, a pale, wasted child. Marx was shattered.

> I have suffered every kind of misfortune [he wrote to Engels] but I have only just learned what real unhappiness is. . . . In the midst of all the suffering which I have lived through in these days, the thought of you, and your friendship, and the hope that we may still have something reasonable to do in this world has kept me upright. . . . Bacon says that really important people have so many contacts with nature and the world, have so much to interest them, that they easily get over any loss. I am not of those important people. My child's death has affected me so greatly that I feel the loss as bitterly as on the first day. My wife is also completely broken down.

The strain affected not only Jenny Marx and the children but

Marx himself. By the time that Musch had died—the official diagnosis was tuberculosis—Marx had a running catarrh, which eventually developed into the tuberculosis of which he too was to die. He began to suffer from insomnia, which led him to a dependence on drugs, readily available and commonly used in the nineteenth century. The most popular was opium, one of the ingredients of the notorious laudanum. A few years later he was reported to be suffering from liver trouble, a gall bladder condition, headaches and neuralgia of the head muscles, inflammation of the eyes, and boils which made life more and more uncomfortable for him. His physical problems were aggravated by a craving for highly seasoned foods and by the enormous number of cigars he smoked. These illnesses were a constant irritation and interfered with his work and his study, for he had now developed the habit of spending ten to twelve hours every day at the reading room of the British Museum. Sitting still was painful because of the boils. In 1858 he wrote Engels, "I am plagued like Job, though not so God-fearing. Everything that these gentlemen [the doctors] say boils down to the fact that one ought to be a prosperous *rentier* and not a poor devil like me, as poor as a church mouse."

The humiliation of life drove him into frenzies of rage and anger and hatred against his enemies, real or imagined. Yet ten years later he could write quite objectively:

> I have sacrified everything I had to the revolutionary battles. I do not regret having done so. Quite to the contrary. If I had to begin my career again, I would do the same. Only I would not get married.
>
> I laugh at the so-called "practical" men and their wisdom. Of course, if one wants to be a swine, one can turn one's back on mankind's torments and worry about one's own skin.

6

Das Kapital,
The Last Great Work

The revolutions had failed across Europe. The 1850s opened with leaders and rebels shot down, hunted, imprisoned, executed, murdered, their survivors labelled enemies of the state. From France to the Russian border, the forces of oppression had won. The proletariat was in disarray; hundreds of thousands of workers, farmers, the unemployed emigrated to the Americas, Africa, the Pacific islands, wherever they could find a life that promised the chance of work and freedom. Marx had foreseen the collapse of the revolts even as they had started, for he

believed the working classes were not ready. But he knew at the
same time that, in the long run, the revolution would succeed
in the inevitable dialectic of history. The struggle was to be
carried on from England, the one country that to him was the
epitome of capitalistic greed and wealth. He reorganized the
Communist League and began to lecture on communist theory
and the theoretical training of the workers. German émigrés
began to straggle in from the continent, men who had fought
the various governments and now would form the core of the
revitalized, hardened, experienced League. Engels, in Manchester, fell into the role of the rising young entrepreneur. He kept
Mary and Lizzie Burns in their little cottage, enjoyed himself
at his club among other businessmen, went riding every day,
much to Marx's annoyance, for Marx wondered why the money
spent on horses could not be put into the revolution instead;
that is, be given to him, but he kept up a steady correspondence
with his collaborator.

For a short period Marx thought that the refugees must form
the core of an active underground committed to carrying on the
revolution by violence and terrorism, and he was willing for the
first time to be intimately involved rather than standing apart
from the fighters. The Prussian agent who infiltrated Marx's
circle in London in 1850 reported to Berlin that there were
three sections in the movement, one open and apparently peaceful; a second intended to create disturbances at the proper time;
and a third, supposedly secret, which was divided into Leaders
and Blindmen, the latter being revolutionaries of great courage
and daring who were reserved for assassinations. Queen Vic-
toria and her family, disguised in Marx's conversation by code
terms (hers was Moon Calf, an old slang term for "abortion"),
were the primary targets in England; on the continent, various
government officials were to be assassinated. The Prussian

Prime Minister passed on the information to the British Foreign Office, which took the matter far less seriously than the Germans.

That Marx was at the time seriously considering violence cannot be doubted. An ex-soldier from Germany named Gustav Techow, who had fought with skill and bravery on the side of the rebels, is known to have been asked by Marx to be a Blindman. Techow refused. In a letter to a friend in Switzerland, in which he independently confirmed the spy's report, he gave a portrait of Marx as he saw him at the time.

> The impression he made on me was that of someone possessing a rare intellectual supremacy. . . . If his heart had matched his intellect, and if he had possessed as much love as hate, I would have gone through fire for him. . . . He was the first and only one among us all [the Communists] to whom I would entrust leadership. . . . Yet it is a matter for regret in view of our aims that this man with his fine intellect is lacking in nobility of soul. I am convinced that a most dangerous personal ambition has eaten away all the good in him. He laughs at the fools who parrot his proletarian catechism [*The Communist Manifesto*]. . . . The only people he respects are the aristocrats, the genuine ones, these who are well aware of their aristocracy. . . . I took away with me the impression that the acquisition of personal power was the aim of all his endeavours.

Marxist sources state that Techow approached Marx to become a member of the revolutionary movement, provided that he could remain both bourgeois and a professional soldier, conditions that Marx would not accept.

The need for sustaining the momentum of 1848 and 1849 seemed crucial to Marx. He and Engels, in their desire for immediate direct action, drew up a program outlined in a short paper now identified by various titles, of which *A Plan of Action*

Against Democracy is the most descriptive. The Plan graphically outlined the task facing the revolutionaries (it was also to serve as one of Lenin's guides during the Russian revolution). Briefly, it said that when the bourgeoisie had come into full control of the state, the proletariat would then be under the illusion that conditions would be better for them too. But the proletariat, which had helped the bourgeoisie to its victory, must now attack its former allies. "It is obvious that bloody fighting lies ahead," warned Marx and Engels. The bourgeoisie, hesitant and indecisive in the mass, and wanting to relax in the fruits of its victory, will expect the same behavior of the workers. But "the armed proletariat" must "dictate such conditions to them that the rule of bourgeois democrats will from the beginning carry the seeds of its own downfall and their subsequent oppression by the rule of the proletariat will be considerably facilitated."

The workers must not relax their agitation following the initial bourgeois victory nor allow it to be suppressed. And a free rein must be given to violence against the new ruling classes and the symbols of the previous one. "Far from opposing the so-called excesses, those examples of popular vengeance against hated individuals or public buildings which have acquired hateful memories, we must not only condone these examples but lend them a guiding hand."

But a direct revolutionary program was beyond Marx, and was to remain so. He turned to the means in which he was trained, and with which he had had experience. With Engels he tried to revive the *Neue Rheinische Zeitung* but could raise only enough money for six issues, which were printed in Germany. Marx's main interest at this time was the uprising in France and the lessons to be learned from it. His long analysis, "The Class Struggle in France," was published in the *Neue Rheinische*

Zeitung. Then, when Louis Napoleon's followers staged a coup in 1851 and made him dictator and then emperor, Marx published another long work, "The Eighteenth Brumaire of Louis Bonaparte," blaming the peasants for what he considered a step backwards. The new Bonaparte dynasty "represents not the enlightenment, but the superstition of the peasant; not his judgment but his prejudice; not his future but his past." He urged the peasants to turn elsewhere for liberation, to "find their natural ally and leader in the urban proletariat, whose task is the overthrow of the bourgeois order." He ended his essay with an attack on the military-bureaucratic machine in France, lamenting that "all revolutions perfected this machine instead of smashing it." The proletarian revolution cannot leave intact this fundamentally exploitative instrument, he stated, but must "concentrate all its forces of destruction against it."

While he was struggling with these intellectually satisfying but economically profitless activities, a small windfall dropped into Marx's hands. The *New York Tribune,* then a socialist, populist, radical newspaper opposed to slavery, asked him to be a correspondent on a weekly basis. It had the largest circulation of any paper in the United States, with some 200,000 sales, and was antagonistic to all of the governments in Europe. The *Tribune*'s editor, Charles Dana, and the chief writer, Albert Brisbane, both followers of the French socialist Charles Fourier, had met Marx in Cologne in 1848 and were deeply impressed by him. They offered one pound sterling per article and gave Marx a free hand to write about what pleased him. However, Marx did not write all of the pieces that bore his byline; about a quarter of them were written by Engels, especially those on military subjects, for Engels was a military buff—his nickname was The General—and in fact it was Engels who wrote the first of the *Tribune* articles, requested by Dana, dealing with the

strategies of the Prussian and Austrian armies during the revolts of 1848. The *Tribune*'s London correspondent became one
of the most popular of the paper's contributors, especially noted
for his knowledge of military affairs, and he was widely quoted
in the United States and abroad. The *Tribune,* in a tribute to
Marx in 1853:

> Mr. Marx has very decided opinions of his own, with some of
> them we are far from agreeing, but those who do not read his
> letters neglect one of the most instructive sources of information
> on the great question of current European politics.

By this time Marx had gained enough confidence in his mas-
tery of English to write directly in it; previously Engels had
translated everything. Not all of the articles, however, were
published; a series by Engels against pan-Slavism and a number
of articles by Marx against Tsarist Russia and French policies
in eastern Europe were rejected; the Marxist-Leninist Institute
has also charged that many of the published articles were edited
or distorted. Nevertheless, Marx poured out a steady stream of
material, ranging far and wide. He analyzed the British state
system, the United States Constitution, electoral system, and
various parties, and attacked the aristocracy and the industrialists. The new French emperor was another popular subject with
him, as were the royalty of the rest of Europe. "The King of
Prussia's Insanity," "The Divine Right of the Hohenzollerns,"
and "Austrian [Hapsburg] Bankruptcy" were some of his top-
ics. The spreading of colonialism furnished the subject for a
number of articles—"The British Rule in India," "History of
the Opium Trade," "Revolution in China and in Europe,"
"Question of the Ionian Islands," "The Excitement in Ireland,"
and "Investigation of Tortures in India." He wrote about the
Crimean War, the colonizing of South America, the Balkans,

the punitive expeditions by the French against the nomads of North Africa—there was no subject too distant or too obscure to excite his interest, concern, and wrath.

He continued the articles for the *Tribune* until 1862, when he had a falling out with the editors over the United States Civil War. They felt he did not understand conditions in the United States; he thought they failed to place the war, the southern plantations, slavery, and northern industry into the context of dialectical materialism. He charged the *Tribune* with allowing sympathizers of the South to control the editorial board and with not supporting the cause of black regiments in the northern armies, for he believed that the presence of such troops would help undermine the power of the slave owners. In the summer of 1862 he wrote to Engels, "A single Nigger regiment would have a remarkable effect on the Southerners' nerves." But by then his usefulness as a foreign correspondent for the *Tribune* had ended.

Meanwhile he was writing for various European publications, eliminating his enemies, real or imagined, from the ranks of the Communists in London, and doing the research for *Das Kapital,* the work that ranks with *The Communist Manifesto* as his other great contribution to radical literature.

His daily toil in the reading room of the British Museum, along with his boils, are probably what are remembered most about Marx's life. Marx would customarily arrive at the museum about nine in the morning with a small group of followers —most of them also shabby or ragged foreigners. Marx would assign chores and reading desks and would work steadily throughout the day until about seven, when the museum closed, after which he would go home for supper and his writing. The only interruptions came when he had meetings or appointments.

The British Museum was a tremendous resource for Marx, for here were not only works in many languages by a wide variety of economists, historians, and philosophers but also the innumerable reports issued by government and private investigating committees concerned with social and working conditions in England at the time. In fact, Marx relied so heavily not only upon the theories of others but the hard digging of the English reformers who went into the slums, mines, factories, and fields to observe conditions firsthand that he drew, years later, a very harsh criticism from George Bernard Shaw. Shaw complained:

> There was nothing about Socialism in the widely read first volume of *Das Kapital*: every reference it made to workers and capitalists showed that Marx had never breathed industrial air, and had dug his case out of bluebooks in the British Museum. Compared with Darwin, he seemed to have no power of observation; there was not a fact in *Das Kapital* that had not been taken out of a book, nor a discussion that had not been opened by somebody else's pamphlet.

Yet Shaw felt obligated to add the important qualifications, "The world is greatly indebted to Marx for his description of the selfishness and stupidity of that respected middle class so worshipped in Germany and England, and *Das Kapital* is one of those books that changes people if they can be persuaded to read it." Shaw adds the interesting comment, "However, it is the work of a man who is not a member of normal German or English society."

Marx had long been thinking about a major work on economics before he actually began *Das Kapital.* He had made some preliminary studies in Paris in 1843 and 1844 of the problems of wages, profits, and rent. By the first month of 1845

Engels had urged him to "get your book on economics finished."

Parts of his studies appeared in various journals, but a finished manuscript was far from forthcoming. In 1851, he estimated that he would have the book completed in five weeks. In 1857, when Europe was experiencing a financial crisis, he felt acutely the urgency of finishing the work. "The damned book," as he called it, began to haunt him. The more he studied, the more complex the project became. What had appeared in scholarly publications was often ignored by the public. The problem, Marx said, was that:

> The huge amount of material piled up in the British Museum, the favorable vantage-point that London offered for studying bourgeois society, and finally the new stage of development that seemed to have been reached with the discovery of gold in California and Australia, all obliged me to start again from the beginning and work critically through the new material. These studies seemed to lead me into quite separate branches of science, in which I was obliged to linger for varying lengths of time.

He would not write about what he did not understand perfectly, and thus he was forced to broaden his work, to explore uncharted territories, which in turn led him into further unknowns. He amassed trunkfuls of notes. A later tenant in one of Marx's London domiciles found a trunk hidden under a stairwell; it was full of writings scribbled in German. The tenant, an Englishman, threw it out; afterwards it was realized that the trunk was one of Marx's with his voluminous notes for some project or other.

At one point he complained to Engels, "I know everything about capital except how to amass it." But there was, strangely for this man who was such a bitter foe of the capitalist system, even an attempt at playing the capitalist. For a year, working with funds he had borrowed or inherited, Marx, as he was finishing *Das Kapital,* plunged heavily into the London stock market, buying and selling with some shrewdness, for he doubled his investments. But in the end he lost everything, not only his profits but his own capital. At last the final words were satisfactorily stated—"the capitalist mode of production and accumulation" and "therefore capitalist private property" have for their fundamental condition nothing but "the annihilation of self-earned private property; in other words, the expropriation of the labourer"—and the great work was completed. On April 2, 1867, Marx wrote Engels that he was about to go to Germany with the manuscript to have the type set. He found that the printer he had contracted for in Hamburg did not have adequate facilities for the book, so he sent it to another printer in Leipzig. It took almost four months to set the massive work, and it finally appeared in print on September 14 in an edition of one thousand copies.

Marx had hoped the book would be a means of solving his financial problems, but at first there seemed to be no readers for it. The solution was to have Engels write a number of reviews, half attacking, half praising the work, for the "bourgeois" press. Nevertheless it was generally ignored by the academic and journalistic world. A year later a young Russian liberal came across it and began to work on a translation. It was not until four years later in the autumn of 1871 that the one thousand German copies were sold. The Russian edition of three thousand appeared in 1872 and was an immediate success. Meanwhile Marx went to work on a revision of the work, and the second German version appeared about the same time as the Russian one, with numerous changes and improvements. A French edition, appearing in 1875, which Marx helped translate, contained his further improvements and was considered by far the best version until Engels issued a fourth German edition in 1890, which is now taken as the final and official version of *Das Kapital.*

Marx had planned another volume, but somehow the completion of the task escaped him. His health had failed seriously, and at the same time the problem of accumulating research seemed to be beyond his control. His requests for material from friends in different countries brought in stacks of books, pamphlets, newspapers, and magazines, and his notebooks grew constantly. He seemed more interested in the research now than in the actual writing, and he went on scribbling away in a handwriting that was virtually illegible, even to Engels. After his death in 1883 a huge bundle of material was found with the succeeding volume of *Das Kapital,* but it was in a chaotic state. There were two separate, raw versions of the second volume and a large number of sketches and notes. There was so much material that Engels realized not one but two volumes would be required, and even the second of these needed two separate parts. Volumes II and III are known as *The Process of Capitalist Circulation* and *The Process of Capitalist Production as a Whole.* Engels spent twelve years in completion of these massive works, but towards the end of that period he realized that there was much more to be included. A section called *A History of Theories of Surplus-Value,* meant for the third volume, was so massive that Engels turned its completion over to a young German radical named Karl Kautsky. Kautsky thought the drafts and notes he had inherited demanded their own existence, and he produced out of them a three-volume work, *Theories of Surplus-Value,* which was published early in this century. Kautsky,

once a Communist hero, was eventually denounced as an opportunist and scoundrel by the Bolsheviks, despite his service
to the cause of explaining Marx to the world.

Das Kapital lays out not only Marx's thinking but Engels's
as well, and is his final statement after thirty-five years of study,
analysis, battles with enemies of every type, and polemics. The
work itself can be read on many levels, depending on one's
interest and orientation. It abounds with Marx's wry, private
jokes, and dismissals of old scores. One example of many will
be sufficient: in warning of the perpetual crisis of capitalism,
"the universal crisis," he says the crisis is returning, "and by
the universality of its theatre and the intensity of its action, it
will drum dialectics even into the heads of the mushroom-
upstarts of the new, holy Prusso-Roman empire."

But to get to more substantial material, it is, to begin with,
a dramatic indictment of nineteenth-century, and even twen-
tieth-century, bourgeois capitalism. The many examples that
Marx has furnished of living conditions among the poor and of
working conditions in the factories and mines drawn directly
from the massive documentation of the British reformers, are
given a special pungency and sharpness by Marx's wrathful
mind. He also drew heavily upon Engels's descriptions of life
in the English mill towns and from similar material supplied by
other friends. It is this kind of imaginative writing that has led
critics to point out the literary qualities of *Das Kapital.* The
essence, of course, is Marx's interpretation of humanity set
against the unfolding of history and the ultimate outcome,
which he sees as nothing more or less than the justification of
the workers and their victory over the forces of evil, the feudal
and bourgeois capitalist lords of the past and present who have
held the workers in servitude. There is almost a messianic
quality to this view, with the worker being his own savior. And

it is a view which, although not a religion, requires faith as much as any heavenly or supernatural doctrine.

In summary, in *Das Kapital,* Marx sees economic conditions as the basis of all life. Political and ideological conditions are only the superstructure above them and change as economic conditions do. Historical stages succeed one another according to the dialectical concept that progress or growth is founded upon conflict, all history being a series of class struggles.

Running through the work is Marx's concept of the worker, of the proletariat, the one social class which produces more wealth than it consumes, this wealth being taken by others who have the means of production because they have access to or own natural resources, factories, machinery, transport, and above all capital or at least credit. With these assets the capitalists control the workers and force them to labor not on their terms but for as little as possible. Of the capitalist Marx states cogently, "Fanatically bent on increasing value, he ruthlessly forces the human race to produce for the sake of production."

The capitalist has created a revolution of his own, Marx says, and in doing so he creates the material conditions for a true basis of a higher form of society.

> The bourgeoisie cannot exist without constantly revolutionizing the instruments of production, and thereby the relations of production and with them the entire relations of society. . . . During its rule of scarcely one hundred years, it has created more massive and colossal productive forces than all the earlier generations taken together. Subjection of the forces of nature to man, application of chemistry and industry to agriculture, steam navigation, railways, the electric telegraph, clearing entire continents for cultivation, canalization of rivers, whole populations conjured up out of the earth—what earlier age had

even a presentiment of such gigantic social forces slumbering in
the lap of socialized labor?

In the revolutions of the seventeenth to the nineteenth centuries, the bourgeoisie constantly sought to develop new means of
production which the feudal system opposed. The age of the
hand-operated weaving loom produced feudal society, while the
age of the steam-driven loom created capitalistic-bourgeois society with its new ideas, forms of religion, and principles. The
bourgeoisie, through its advanced technical methods, overthrew the feudal class, which was bound to a narrow economic
system. The newly developed capitalism, with its dynamism
and ruthlessness, accelerated production to a new degree. But
each stage of production would soon be outmoded as the capitalists developed more advanced technology. However, capitalism is its own gravedigger, for while it is enriching itself, it is
also producing an implacable enemy, the proletariat, which will
in turn overthrow the bourgeoisie as soon as the capitalistic
organization of production becomes outmoded in relation to
the requirements of productive forces. The stage for the final
struggle in this evolutionary chain, says *Das Kapital,* is now at
hand. The result will be a victory for the proletariat and their
control of production and distribution, followed by the eventual
withering away of the state, as we know it now, and an eventual
classless society. The process is inevitable, but it is to be speeded
up by unifying the proletariat wherever it is to be found, by
working with any political force useful for the moment, and
sooner or later by resorting to revolution.

One of the underlying themes is that of surplus value, the
means by which capital produces more capital. Simply put, in
one of Marx's examples, a person who works for twenty days
receives pay for only ten, the surplus labor being used not only

to pay off the cost of raw materials and machinery and other overhead but to produce a profit. Thus the capitalist accumulates capital, part of which he keeps, part of which goes to the stockholders, and part of which is used to enlarge his instruments of production in an apparently never-ending movement upwards.

But there are weaknesses in the system as Marx sees it. As great monopolies grow and the bourgeois capitalists constantly revolutionize their forces of production with better and better machinery, twin forces of destruction are at work. First, the more the machine replaces human labor, the lower will be the surplus value and the lower the profit, for surplus value depends on the living worker not a mechanical replacement. The group of capitalists at the summit becomes smaller and at the same time more powerful, while the proletariat, discontented and frustrated, is enlarged. Second, the unlimited struggle between capitalists for world markets becomes increasingly intense, for they are tied to a system of unfettered competition in which they must overtake and destroy their rivals.

Furthermore, Marx points out that as capitalism goes through its series of revolutions of growth and competition, depressions inevitably result, growing more and more international and acute. Wars are waged on a greater and greater scale in order to gain new markets, to secure them, or to defend them. Marx was able to condense the process and its outcome into a single paragraph.

> While there is a progressive diminution in the number of capitalist magnates, there is of course a corresponding increase in the mass of poverty, enslavement, degeneration and exploitation, but at the same time there is a steady intensification of the role of the working class—a class which grows ever more numerous,

and is disciplined, unified and organized by the very mechanism
of the capitalist method of production which has flourished with
it and under it. The centralization of the means of production
and the socialization of labor reach a point where they prove
incompatible with their capitalist husk. This bursts asunder.
The knell of private property sounds. The expropriators are
expropriated.

Marx admitted that the revolution could be carried out "entirely by peaceful and legal means," but, as has been seen, he
thought a bloody revolution was inevitable. At any rate, once
the workers were in control there would be unity between the
producers (the workers) and the conditions of production,
which would no longer be alienated from the people. Production would become organized and planned in order to provide
for the full and free development of every individual. Marx
realized, however, that there still would be surplus value, but
in this case it would be employed for the benefit of the workers;
for the surplus would be used to maintain a higher standard of
living and to create new means of production, which would
insure new jobs and shorten hours for the present workers. How
is this surplus to be distributed to individuals? Marx realized
that people's capacities and needs are unequal, so, as the famous
phrase goes, the profits, or rewards, would accrue "to everyone
according to his need, from everyone according to his
capacity." What he saw was:

a community of free individuals, carrying on their work with the
means of production in common, in which the labor-power of
all the different individuals is consciously applied as the com-
bined labor-power of the community. . . . The total product of
our community is a social product. One portion serves as fresh
means of production and remains social. But another portion is
consumed by the members as means of subsistence.

When this vision of the future harmonious world of the proletariat—on earth and not in heaven—finally was absorbed, filtered, and simplified, *Das Kapital* became, as Engels was to remark, "the Bible of the masses," with all the hopes, aspirations, dreams of rewards, explanations for personal sorrow and misery, and the touch of mysticism that the term Bible implies. Meanwhile, we must turn back to some more prosaic events in Marx's life, for running side by side with this revolutionary and seminal work were the daily problems of family and friends and of the battles in which he was engaged in building a solidly based and obedient party of hard-core revolutionaries.

While *Das Kapital* was being completed, Marx's personal crisis continued unabated. His chief sources of money, aside from the small but steady payments for the *Tribune* articles, were Engels, his mother, and various relatives and friends. He was a constant drain upon the uncomplaining Engels, who was willing to make whatever sacrifices necessary to support Marx and his family. Engels himself had no family other than Mary Burns, to whom he was deeply attached. When she died in 1863, Marx's reaction was one of indifference, and in the letter which should have commiserated with Engels, he instead complained of his own problems.

> If I don't get a larger sum, our household here can hardly survive another two weeks. It is abominably egotistical of me to tell you of these horrors just at the moment. . . . But one trouble cures another. And, after all, what am I to do? In the whole of London there is not a single man to whom I can speak my heart freely, and in my own house I play the silent Stoic in order to counter outbreaks from the other side.

And he added, "If only, instead of Mary, [it had been] my mother, who anyhow is now full of physical infirmities and has lived a fair span of life."

Engels and Marx, and Marx's daughters, London, the 1860s.

Engels was understandably annoyed at Marx's reaction. "You will not be surprised that this time my own misfortune and your frosty reply made it quite impossible for me to answer you before," he wrote Marx, for all his friends, even the most bourgeois, had shown him far more sympathy than he had received from Marx. The quarrel was patched up, and Engels continued to send money. Marx made a trip the summer of the same year to see his mother, reporting to Engels, "There is no hope of any cash from my mother. She is rapidly approaching her end. But she has destroyed a number of promissory notes which I gave her earlier." His mother did not die until the end of 1863, leaving him a moderate sum of money. Marx did not tell Engels how much he had inherited, probably for fear that Engels might want to be repaid some of the considerable sums he had given the Marxes. And about the same time Marx received a legacy from his old friend Wilhelm Wolff, who had died in Manchester. His total inheritance from his mother and Wolff was about thirty thousand marks. The money came to him in the summer of 1864. The Marxes moved to a larger house in London, but a year later he was forced to return to the pawnshop and to beg money again of Engels. In one letter he stated that he had been unable to earn a single cent—"Altogether I am living above my means"—and apologized for the middle-class manner in which the family had recently been living. He had "at least [to] make it up to them for a short while." He added, "A purely proletarian set-up would not be right here, though this might be all very well if my wife and I were alone or the girls were young." He wrote that "the tradesmen are menacing; some of them have cut off our credit and threatened to sue." He had come to resent his dependence upon Engels, and privately Marx and his wife built up a deep anger towards him; Laura Marx later destroyed a number of letters in which Marx and his wife had made disparaging remarks about Engels.

Meanwhile Engels, having buried Mary Burns, now took her sister Lydia (called Lizzie or Lizzy) as his new mistress. Lizzie had lived with Engels and Mary, so the shift in household arrangements was probably not too traumatic for either of them. Like her sister Mary, Lizzie was an Irish nationalist and the Engels household often sheltered members of the Sinn Fein, the underground revolutionary Irish movement. When Lizzie Burns died in January, 1879, Engels took in her niece Mary Ellen as his housekeeper and made her his heir.

Marx and latter-day Communists have been very reticent about Engels's personal affairs and either pretended that Engels had married the Burns sisters in turn or that they did not exist. At any rate, Marx and Engels stood at opposite ends of the spectrum in their opinions about the family and sex. Engels was open and free about the institution (one of his most interesting works is *The Origin of the Family,* in which he predicts complete sexual freedom), while Marx stood by the most puritanical standards of his age. And yet, in one of the most well-kept secrets of the revolution, he was found to be the father of a child born to his wife's maid, the long-suffering, hardworking Helene Demuth. The baby, a boy named Freddie, was spirited away and placed in an English family, where he grew up a typical English workman, lower middle class, responsible and interested in his job (he was a skilled fitter and turner), his union, and his friends but not the revolution. He never married, but had an illegitimate son named Harry, who eventually ran away. One of Marx's biographers, Robert Payne, was able to locate people who knew Freddie Demuth. He was said to be quiet and meticulous, somewhat above the average workman. "Uncle Fred," said the son in a household where he lived, "was

Engels's mistress, the Irish factory girl, Lizzie Burns.

a neat, dapper little chap with bright-blue eyes and a thick mustache. When his hair started to turn gray, he used to scrape walnut shells to make a reddish dye, and he dyed his hair and mustache with it. He was very quick in his movements and smiled a lot. He always held himself upright, and when he went to work he always carried a gladstone bag, and I had the feeling it was empty. It was just something he liked to carry. He always wore a Muller hat—something like a derby—which workmen didn't wear very often. They wore caps."

Marx is known to have visited his son at least once, secretly, and Marx's daughter Eleanor became his close friend; some of her letters to Freddie have survived. He died in 1929, mourned by his fellow workers as a good craftsman and responsible citizen, totally unlike those radical artisans Bauer, Schapper, and Moll who had founded the London branch of the League of the Just three quarters of a century earlier. This scandal, along with Marx's dissemblance in financial dealings with Engels, and his resentment towards his collaborator and Engels's free style of living with the Burns sisters, are all missing in official Communist literature.

7

The International

During most of the period in which he had been working on *Das Kapital* in London, up to 1864, Marx had abstained from any kind of political activity. Ferdinand Lassalle, two years earlier, had tried to enlist his help in a new workers' movement in Germany, but he had refused to get involved. Marx and Lassalle had always been close friends. They had maintained contact since they had first met during the 1848 Revolution, and Lassalle had contributed to the fund which had enabled Marx and his family to flee to England. Lassalle came from

Silesia, in eastern Germany. He was Jewish, rich (and thus the subject of some nasty anti-Semitic remarks by both Marx and Engels), highly urbane, and free with money. But he was also one of the leading radicals on the continent, and his natural talents of leadership, his easy romantic manner, and his ability to proclaim his ideas to crowds were an affront to Marx, who, nevertheless, was from time to time dependent upon Lassalle. He was not only a popular orator but a skilled organizer, and fearless as a revolutionary. One assumes that Marx must have felt himself very stodgy and rather envious of Lassalle's natural talents.

When Marx, Engels, and most of the other German revolutionary leaders went into exile, Lassalle remained behind to organize the workers into a better and more active proletarian movement. He was arrested several times but was always released.

Lassalle's success as a leader in the absence of the exiled men led him to regard himself as a kind of benevolent dictator over the workers, for they lacked the intellectual and political skills he possessed. Though Marx and Engels were forced to respect Lassalle's courage and his ability to reach the workers, they also made fun of him, for they thought that aside from the theories he had picked up from Marx, he was hopelessly impractical. For example, he developed the idea that there could be an alliance between the aristocracy, the army, and the proletariat against the bourgeoisie, the result being a collective state run for the benefit of the workers. Marx and Engels said the theory was ridiculous. Lassalle's successes irritated Marx, and he refused to join any movement his rival initiated. By 1864 Lassalle's work in Germany had reached a peak. He had founded dozens of workers' cooperatives, which were extremely radical but also extremely nationalistic. Changing his theories, Lassalle now thought that the workers could advance their cause by collaborating for the time with their natural enemies, the bourgeoisie. This kind of opportunism infuriated Marx, who had been saying that one of the reasons for the failures of the 1848 uprisings was that the workers in the different countries had joined forces with their employers, the bourgeoisie, against the crowns of Europe. Later Marx subscribed to such an alliance himself, but under terms he himself dictated.

Meanwhile Lassalle became more and more powerful, and he posed a real threat to Marx and Marx's influence on the continent. Marx's anger increased steadily. In April he wrote Engels about "Itzig" (as he referred to Lassalle) and his battle with the "Workers' Central Committee for the Leipzig Workers' (for this read Louts') Congress," saying, "His attitude—very important—flinging about phrases borrowed from us—is quite that of the future workers' dictator." Engels thought the situation in Germany was "beginning to get unpleasant." In another letter (of many irritable ones) Marx wrote, "The same Itzig otherwise also collects in his manure factory the party excrements we dropped twenty years ago, with which world history is to be fertilized."

The situation was complicated and had many shades of political inferences. Aside from the dubious question of enlisting the crown and the army to aid the proletariat against the bourgeoisie, an idea which Lassalle apparently did not actually try to put into practice, he also made a strenuous and fairly successful effort to detach many of the workers from the vast mass of liberals, bourgeoisie especially, who opposed the state. Lassalle thought the doctrine preached in *The Communist Manifesto,* that the bourgeoisie should be supported during its own revolution, incorrect, for the German middle class was not at all revolutionary. He wanted a specifically working-class

Engels in the 1860s, the rising entrepreneur and sportsman.

party, standing by itself, which would make the others, whatever their liberalism, look like a "reactionary mass." So, Lassalle and his supporters had the reputation at the time of being
the most radical of all groups in Germany. Suddenly the conflict between Marx and Lassalle was ended, after a summer of
letters between Marx and Engels complaining about their rival.
Lassalle was killed in a duel over a woman, a romantic adven-
ture that was further proof to Marx of Lassalle's impracticality
in the face of the revolution. Early in September, 1864, Engels
wrote to Marx:

> What rejoicing will reign among the factory owners and the
> Progressive swine—Lasalle was after all the only chap they were
> afraid of in Germany itself.

And Marx replied:

> After all he was still one of the old guard and the enemy of our
> enemies. And then the thing came as such a surprise that it is
> now hard to believe such a noisy, "stirring," "pushing" person
> is now as dead as a mouse and has got to keep his mouth shut
> "altogether."

A few weeks after Lassalle's death Marx turned again to
active politics. Without his help the most radical of the workers
of England and France had founded an organization to further
their interests. The movement was almost spontaneous among
these artisans. At a joint meeting in London on September 28,
1864, they inaugurated an organization called The Working
Men's International Association. The title was quickly shortened to the International, and the organization was known by
that name afterwards. The International covered a wide range
of radical and liberal beliefs, and its initial purpose was one of
creating harmony among workers in their common struggle.

But that vague hope soon disappeared, for Marx, who did not
attend the first meeting, was elected as one of the thirty-two
men in the Central Committee, whose initial role was to draw
up a constitution. Marx played no part in the first attempts;
then he intervened on October 18, inviting the other delegates
to his house for a meeting. The talk dragged on all night without any decisions, and in weariness the others turned the project
over to Marx. From then on, until he dissolved the organization, Marx was the voice of the International. The Preamble of
the Provisional Rules was simple Marxism, "The emancipation
of the working classes must be achieved by the working classes
themselves. . . . "

And the program continued from there along the lines that
Marx had already established in his writings. The goal of the
working class was to abolish all class rule. Political struggle by
the working class against the ruling classes was the means of
emancipating the working people from oppression by the capitalist system, which was based on their economic subjugation
by those who owned the means of production. Unity of forces
on class lines and proletarian internationalism were vital principles for the working-class movement. Marx noted some gains
recently—the work day had been reduced to ten hours—but in
the end, as in the beginning, "To conquer political power has
therefore become the great duty of the working classes."

In the beginning the International was a true international,
for it included men from a wide variety of radical groups from
all the nations of Europe, who were influenced by all shades of
socialist doctrines. They included not only utopian socialists
who wanted a peaceful evolution but also anarchists who
sought a quick demolition of the remnants of feudalism and of
the new capitalism by violence in order to rebuild society. In

Marx, aged 43, at the height of his intellectual powers.

the beginning, contrary to his usual dictatorial manner, Marx worked quietly and efficiently and with great understanding of the various and often contradictory shades of opinion. But these apparent concessions were given only until he gained control over the group and established his own position. However, he never attended any of the yearly meetings, except for the last, and he rarely came even to the weekly and monthly meetings. His work was primarily behind the scenes, drawing up programs and manifestos and carrying on correspondence. He was confident of the success of what he was doing. In September, 1867, he wrote Engels, "Things are moving. And in the next revolution, which is perhaps nearer than it appears, *we* (i.e., you and I) will have this powerful engine *in our hands.*" He added that he thought the various major factions, among them those that followed the ideas of Proudhon, Lassalle, and the Italian revolutionary, Mazzini, would destroy each other.

Meanwhile he directed the International to some of the basic problems facing the proletariat, among them the questions of hours, child labor, women in the work force, trade unions, education of the workers, relations of the proletariat with the state, and the use of political force. Conventions were held yearly at a major city, starting with London (1865), followed by Geneva (1866), Lausanne (1867), Brussels (1868), and Basel (1869). Marx was able to handle or absorb opposition from all sources but one, and that was Mikhail Bakunin, who had finally come back to western Europe in 1864 after escaping from exile in Siberia. When Bakunin turned up in London, Marx wrote to Engels about him, "Seeing him again after sixteen years, I find that he is one of the few people who have gone forwards and not back." In a moment of misjudgment Marx invited Bakunin to become a member of the International. Bakunin wrote to Marx, "My Fatherland is now the International, of which you are the most important founder. So you see, my dear friend, that I am a pupil of yours, and proud to be one."

But the tension slowly built up between them. Five years later Bakunin wrote to another Russian, the noted essayist and radical Alexander Herzen, that while Marx had tremendous talents and insight, still, "I might have to quarrel with him. Not of course attack him personally, but quarrel with him over a matter of principle, namely State Communism which he advocates so strongly, as do the Germans and Englishmen he leads. That could be a life and death struggle."

Bakunin, like Proudhon before him and Alexander Kropotkin after him, thought that men are socialists by nature, given the chance, but the state is a coercive machine that perpetuates economic inequalities. Marxist communism, he thought, concentrated all power in the hands of the state and consequently led to the centralization of property in the hands of the state. He told Herzen:

> I desire the abolition of the State. I want to root out completely that principle of authority in the State by which men have always been enslaved, oppressed, exploited and humiliated.

Marx, of course, believed that the state would eventually wither away in a classless society; Bakunin did not think it would, and was sure that the worker would merely be substituting one harsh exploitative master for another. Therefore, the state had to be abolished at the beginning of the revolution. Years later, after Marx's death, Engels wrote a friend that Marx "had proclaimed the abolition of the state, long before there were any anarchists at all."

The struggle intensified, and by 1872, when it was time for the International Congress to be held at The Hague, Marx wrote a friend in almost the same words that Bakunin had used earlier. He said, "At this Congress it will be a question of the very life and death of the International. And before I retire I will at least protect it from destruction."

Sixty-four delegates from Europe were to attend the meeting. There was an American representative, but Marx did not allow him to be seated for he feared the man might sympathize with Bakunin. An Englishman, who had never been in the United States, claimed to represent the city of Chicago, but Marx denounced him as a middle-class quack, a bogus reformer, and a proponent of free love and spiritualism; with this damnation hanging over him, the Englishman too lost his seat. There were six known supporters of Bakunin, but Bakunin himself and the Italian contingent, who were known to favor him, did not appear. Many of the rest of the group had been hand-picked by Marx and Engels, but some of the others, especially among the English, Dutch, Swiss, Belgian, and Spanish delegates, resented Marx's dictatorial manner.

The meeting became a noisy shouting match between the Marxists and the anti-Marxists. The General Council—that is, Marx, for he controlled it—was denounced as being unnecessary; the International could survive without its crushing rule, said his opponents. But the Marxists claimed that a central governing body was a necessity. Meanwhile, in a flood of invective from Engels and from Marx's men, Bakunin was voted out of the International. Then Marx made what seemed like a strange move. Through Engels, he proposed that the headquarters of the International be moved to New York. Marx sat quietly, almost impassively, on the platform listening to the arguments rage about him, for the same handful of his enemies feared that with the headquarters so far away, the organization would fall into the hands of journalists, people who were not workers. And then, while Marx looked on with benign neutral-

After Marx dissolved the International, a Second International was formed. Here Engels (center) presides at a meeting.

ity, the motion was carried by his supporters that the General Council be moved to the United States. That was to be the end of it, for, as Marx wanted, the International began to fade into oblivion and was formally dissolved four years later. The International had served Marx's purposes. It had been extremely useful as a conduit for his ideas. It boasted of seven million members—the police set the figure at five million—and there were at least 800,000 on the records. But it had reached the point where its sheer size made it hard to control, and Marx now feared that it would be taken over by his enemies.

But a radical movement of such size and intensity would not waste away into oblivion. A Second International, socialist and not communist in purpose, was founded in 1889 for nonrevolutionary parties, of which the Germans and the Russians were the most numerous. The British branch, which became the Labour Party, included Sidney Webb, George Bernard Shaw, and Beatrice Potter among its early members (they formed the nucleus of the Fabian Society, a socialist group). It advocated social reform by evolution and worked for nationalization of banks, transport, power, mines, and utilities, and for better housing, shorter work hours, unemployment aid, and self-goverment for the Empire's colonies. The Labour Party was able to win enough votes on several occasions to be elected to power, and many of its programs have been obtained. Most of the colonies went further than self-government and are now independent.

In Russia a strong left-wing minority, the Bolsheviks, split off from the Second International, overthrew the moderates (the Mensheviks), who had ousted the Tsar, and established the Third International under the auspices of the new Russian Soviet Republic. The Second International slowly lost its influence, while the Third became the central organization for the Communist parties of the world. During World War II the Third International was dissolved by the Russians as a gesture of good will towards their allies. A so-called Fourth International, founded by Leon Trotsky, the Russian communist dissident, never fully took root, disappearing with his death in 1940.

Bakunin's ideas, as well as those of Proudhon and other early anarchists, continued in various forms. They found support from the Russian noblemen Prince Peter Kropotkin and Count Leo Tolstoi, the novelist. Many of the anarchists turned to violence on the theory that only when the social structure was totally destroyed could a new form of society be established. Even the successive series of revolutions proclaimed by the Marxists were senseless if society was essentially wrong to begin with. One of Bakunin's disciples, Sergei Netchayev, in his *Revolutionary Catechism,* claimed that the doctrine of "propaganda by action" was the only means of advancing the cause of the

revolution. He stated that spectacular assassinations and bomb-
ings were the most effective means of directing the people's
attention to the cause of revolution. Anarchists murdered a
number of world leaders in the nineteenth and early twentieth
centuries, and there are self-proclaimed anarchists at large today working in the same violent tradition, especially in Europe.
But not all anarchists go to such extremes. Under the form of
syndicalism (or anarcho-syndicalism) anarchist doctrines had a
powerful influence in Europe up to the time of World War II.
Some of the most politically and militarily effective forces in the
Spanish Civil War were the various anarchist groups supporting the government. In general the more moderate anarchists
rejected all political and parliamentary effort and sought to use
direct or "industrial" action by the workers against the ruling
classes. The strike was the principle weapon, and a general
strike was to be the means of bringing down the government
and effecting the final revolution. Then the trade unions (not the
state, as Marx taught) would take over the factories and the
other means of production and run them on cooperative principles. The state would no longer exist, being replaced by a federation of unions. Thus there would be no central authority
geographically, but instead a system of "pluralistic authority"
and "functional economic organization."

Ruthless in dealing with enemies, real or suspected, Marx
was also ruthless in trying to take credit for revolutionary and
radical ideas and movements that others had originated. The
Paris Commune, which followed the Franco-Prussian war of
1870, was just such a case. The Parisians spontaneously arose
to defend their city against the enemy, first the Prussians and
then the French provisional government, which had surrendered to the Germans. An official Marxist version, stated by the
Marxist-Leninist Institute, is that Marx "was a direct partici-

pant in the mass revolutionary struggle. . . . It was he who
mainly inspired the working class to independent action during
the war . . . and helped to work out the tactical line of the
proletarian forces in both the belligerent and the neutral countries." The Marx-Engels correspondence and the indecision of
their followers show that they were surprised by the events that
led to the Commune, and while it existed, looked upon it unfa-
vorably, though they tried to reach certain of its leaders with
advice, as they saw the situation from London.

The Commune was an end product of the Franco-Prussian
war, a war waged by the ruling classes of two bourgeois nations
still marked with strong touches of feudalism. At stake were not
only national pride but huge tracts of land, Alsace and Lor-
raine, and the domination of Europe. The French suffered a
tragic defeat at Verdun in 1870, and the emperor, Louis Napoleon III, was taken prisoner. The German armies rolled up to
the gates of Paris. The city resisted, suffering terrible privations.
From a distance Marx could observe the tragedy but could not
put it into perspective. There was constant wrangling among
the members of the International: were they to support Germany, or France, or neither? Should they denounce all wars as
forms of capitalism, or just this war? Or should they accept it
as a stage in the historical process of disintegration of the
bourgeois states?

Meanwhile, the remnant of the French government, in exile
in Bordeaux, signed an armistice with the enemy in January,
1871, surrendering Alsace-Lorraine and agreeing to the payment of a cash indemnity, crushing in its size. The seeds of
another war, to break out in 1914, were thus sown. France
seemed to be prepared to restore the Empire, but the tragedy
and humiliation of conquest by the Prussians released forces

hitherto quiet. In Paris and other cities groups of people, ordinary people—workers, artisans, intellectuals, clerks, among them a few socialists—took over their local governments in the absence of their former officials, who were still in hiding. From the beginning the Paris government, immediately known as the Commune, attempted to follow legal procedures. Proper elections were held and laws observed and passed. The treasury, which could have been opened to get funds for food and arms, was respected. The Provisional government, which had disgracefully surrendered to the Prussians, now attacked the Commune. For two months Paris was besieged. Meanwhile Marx and Engels passed the time in frustrating indecision, their attempts at long range leadership ignored, for the Communards

The Communards battle government troops in Paris. Marx rejected the movement but later tried to take credit for it.

had no interest in outside interference in their struggle to fend off the enemy and to keep the city functioning. The Provisional government finally overwhelmed the under-armed, starving Communards. Tens of thousands—the estimate has reached 100,000—were slaughtered in the week of repression that followed.

What might have passed as a tragic incident in an unfortunate war was now mythologized by Marx into a major revolutionary event. He hailed the Commune as the "incubation of a new society." He proclaimed that the Commune was the first example of the "dictatorship of the Proletariat" which would permit the transition to the classless society. He wrote:

> It was essentially a working-class government, the product of a struggle of the producing against the appropriating class, the political form at last discovered under which to work out the emanicipation of labour.

Later he had the honesty to admit (though only in private) to a Dutch socialist:

> Apart from the fact that this was merely the rising of a town under exceptional conditions, the majority of the Commune was in no sense socialist, nor could it be.

Engels, trying to steer a middle course, hoping the communists would get the credit without literally claiming it, said the Commune was "without any doubt the child of the International intellectually, although the International did not lift a finger to produce it."

But Marx's analysis of the Commune, *The Civil War in France,* was to have far-reaching effects. Lenin took what he wanted from Marx's mythological view of the Commune, made it the model for the October Revolution in Russia, and found

in the pages of *The Civil War in France* much of the Bolshevik
theory of the state.

In 1872 Marx was fifty-six, a respectable age but hardly old.
He had behind him a stormy yet productive life. He had laid
down general principles which were to shake the world, though
how dynamic they would be, Marx could not foresee. Though
tired with the struggle and in a painful state of health, he could
now face life with tranquillity. He was an honored sage of the
revolution, the object of adulation by radicals all over the
world. His name was being invoked, for good or evil, probably
more than any other of his century and possibly, with one or
two exceptions, more than any in all centuries. Engels, in London since 1870, was able to provide the Marxes with a steady
subsidy. The dismal poverty of the past thirty-five years was
over, and Marx could study in peace and receive people in
better surroundings, like any middle-class citizen. The completion of *Das Kapital* seemed to escape him, but the works and
drafts piled up. There was no great necessity to press onward
at all hours as in the past. He was even able to take a broader
view of his own work and his own ideas and could admit that
there was more than one path leading to socialism and that
perhaps revolution was not inevitable in certain countries like
England and Holland and other "advanced" countries.

His family had grown up, but the aura of tragedy that had
always seemed to envelop the Marxes continued. Their daughter Laura married a French radical named Paul Lafargue; he
was the scion of a wealthy Creole family from Cuba. (Marx,
enjoying his customary racial slurs, called his son-in-law Ne-
grillo and Gorilla). Now, not only had Marx seen three of his
own children die, but he witnessed the early deaths of all three
of the Lafargues'. His other daughter Jenny married a radical
journalist, the French socialist Charles Longuet, much to

A last photograph of Marx, taken a few months before his death.

Marx's distress—he once remarked to Engels that he thought both of his sons-in-law were idiots, for "Longuet is the last of the Proudhonists and Lafargue the last of the Bakuninists."

In December, 1881, Frau Marx died, and Marx felt tremendously bereaved. Her death was a blow that he could not overcome. His own health deteriorated, and his mind began to show signs of fatigue and confusion. He wrote a friend:

> I have emerged from my last illness crippled in a two-fold manner: morally through the death of my wife, and physically because I am left with a thickening of the pleura and an increased sensitivity of the trachea. I shall have to sacrifice a certain amount of time in various manoeuvres to restore my health.

In 1882 he went into a year of wandering, visiting France, Algiers, and Switzerland, returning home and going off again. He felt he was slipping. He noted in a letter to his family that his spelling and grammar were bad—"I'm so muddled." Then he complained, "How pointless and empty life is, but how desirable!" Then in January, 1883, his daughter Jenny Longuet died suddenly. It was a further blow to Marx. Two months later, on March 14, Marx himself passed away while sitting in an armchair. Engels could note objectively:

> Perhaps medical skill might have been able to procure him a few more years of vegetative existence, the life of a helpless creature. It might have been a triumph for the doctors that he did not die suddenly, but instead he would have died by inches. And our poor Marx could never have borne that. . . .

As for Engels, along with his collaboration with Marx, he turned out a profusion of writings, running from the pseudonymous articles for the *New York Tribune* to many pamphlets, essays for European publications, and books of his own. One of his most remarkable features was a three-part essay called "The Housing Question." Engels saw the ownership of property as a detriment to the advancement of the proletariat. "The ownership of house, garden and field, and security of tenure in dwelling place," wrote Engels, "is becoming today, under the rule of large-scale industry, not only the worst hindrance to the worker, but the greatest misfortune for the whole working class." To create the modern revolutionary class of the proletariat, "it was absolutely necessary to cut the umbilical cord which still bound the worker of the past to the land." It is the fortunate character of modern large-scale industry that "has turned the worker, formerly chained to the land, into a completely propertyless proletarian, liberated from all traditional fetters and *free as a bird.*" The only answer for the problems of the proletariat was not to go back and give the workers "hearth and home," which would make them into "just such narrowminded, crawling, sneaking slaves as their great-grandfathers were" but as Marx had preached day in and out, "nothing but revolution." And he refers the reader to the first volume of *Das Kapital.*

Like Marx with his voluminous notes for the completion of *Das Kapital,* Engels too became mired in a parallel work, to be called *Dialectics of Nature,* which he never completed because the more crucial *Das Kapital* made a more insistent call upon his time. It was assembled later by the Englishman J.B.S. Haldane from Engels's drafts and notes, written in a curious polyglot tongue. Two examples.

> Wenn Coulomb von particles of electricity spricht, which repel each other inversely as the square of the distance, so nimmt Thomson das ruhib hins als bewiesen.
>
> In der heutigen Gesellechaft, dans le méchanisme civilisé,

Engels in 1888, now an aged and respected revolutionary elder.

Active to the end, Engels speaks on behalf of international communism at a May Day Demonstration in London's Hyde Park.

herrscht duplicité d'action, contrariété de l'interêt individuel avec le collectif; es ist une queue universelle des individus contre les masses.

Someone remarked that "Engels stutters in twenty languages." Besides all the languages of Europe, which he spoke fluently, he knew Russian and some other Slavic tongues, Persian, Old Norse, Anglo-Saxon, Frisian, Gaelic, Danish, Serbian, and Bulgarian, and various related languages, any of which he would drop casually into his works. "Engels was probably the most widely educated man of his day," remarked Haldane in his preface to *Dialectics of Nature*.

What his contribution to the literary world as well as to the revolution might have been we can never know. He spent an inordinate amount of time working with Marx and salvaged the undigestible mass of the second and third volumes of *Das Kapi-*

tal for the workers. Towards the end of his life he tried to put Marx and himself into some kind of perspective.

> I cannot deny that both before and during my forty years' collaboration with Marx I had a certain independent share in laying the formulations, and more particularly in elaborating the theory. But the greater part of its leading basic principles, particularly in the realm of economics and history, and, above all, its final, clear formulation, belong to Marx. What I contributed—at any rate with the exception of a few special studies —Marx could very well have done without me. What Marx accomplished I would not have achieved. Marx stood higher, saw further, and took a wider and quicker view than all the rest of us. Marx was a genius; we others were at best talented. Without him the theory would not be what it is today. It therefore rightly bears his name.

And in another place:

> When one has the good fortune to work for forty years with a man like Marx, one does not usually get the recognition one thinks one deserves during his lifetime. Then if the greater man dies, the lesser easily gets overrated, and this seems to me to be just my case at present; history will set all this right in the end and by that time one will be safely round the corner and know nothing more about anything.

After Marx's death, his surviving daughters, Eleanor and Laura, were to experience more tragedy in their own lives. Eleanor had become involved with Edward Aveling, an English writer, scientist and politician. He was a protégé of Engels, but despite this, was widely disliked for his casual exploitation of friends, especially of women, and his lack of scruples. Eleanor's affair with Aveling lasted fifteen years; for most of this period she lived in anguished despair. The socialist writer Beatrice

Potter, one of the early members of the Second International and of the Fabian Society, recorded her meeting with Eleanor as follows:

> In her person she is comely, dressed in a slovenly picturesque way, with curly black hair flying in all directions. Fine eyes full of life and sympathy, otherwise ugly features and expression, and complexion showing the signs of an unhealthy excited life, kept up with stimulants and tempered by narcotics.

Miss Potter thought Eleanor "lives alone." Eleanor imagined she was a liberated woman, but she had merely fallen into Aveling's Edwardian clutches. Engels, who had the pleasures of the Burns sisters to look back upon (and was now involved with a series of women, especially Austrian) encouraged the affair. But by 1898, Engels was dead, and Eleanor, with little emotional support except from her half brother Freddie Demuth, had reached an end. Aveling was tired of her and had secretly married an actress half his age, though he still shared a house with Eleanor. He now staged a macabre event that might have come from a Soho stage. Pretending to be ill in bed, he talked Eleanor into a suicide pact. He sent the maid out to buy some prussic acid "for the dog." The details of what happened are unknown, but the implications that appeared at the inquest have led scholars to assume the following events. Aveling persuaded Eleanor to take the acid first. Then, as she lay dying, he quickly dressed and went to his office where he made an issue of the time of his arrival and spent the day talking to people. Meanwhile, the maid, who had gone to the druggist's again, returned to find Eleanor alone and near death, an obvious suicide. Aveling was an uncooperative, hostile witness at the inquest, and left many questions unanswered and vague.

Laura and Paul Lafargue, too, suffered unhappy deaths. Lafargue, once so wealthy from his family's sugar plantations, lost his money. In 1911 he and Laura were virtually destitute; they decided that suicide was the only solution. Of Marx's children, only Jenny had what might be called a happy life, though she had died at an early age. She and her husband Charles Longuet had three sons, one a socialist (but not a Marxist), the others a doctor and a journalist. The latter was written off as being very bourgeois. A daughter, also named Jenny, never married. Robert Payne was able to trace Marx's surviving descendants, all French citizens.

> The third generation of Marx's descendants include a sculptor, a landscape painter, a planter in Madagascar, an automobile salesman, and a socialist lawyer, Robert-Jean, who never married. He was the last of the revolutionary descendants. Today [1968] there are fourteen descendants of Marx, all living in France.

Marx was buried in a grave in London's Highgate Cemetery; it was also the resting place of the remains of Jenny von Westphalen, their daughter Eleanor, their grandson Harry Longuet, and the faithful servant Helene Demuth. The site was in an area "normally reserved for persons rejected by official society and the church," notes the Marxist-Leninist Institute. Later the Soviet government installed a marble shrine atop the grave, surmounted by a massive head of Marx which makes him look more like a gentle old cigar maker than the Red Revolutionary Doctor whose ideas were to topple so many governments. Engels's ashes were thrown into the ocean at Eastbourne, to be gently carried by the currents and thrown upon the shores of those same governments.

The death of any man is tragic, but what of the death of many, of millions? I must close on a somewhat personal note, with a memory I have mentioned elsewhere. A young Indian Marxist once spoke to me angrily, hopefully, of the revolution that would sweep his own country. "It is inexorable, inevitable," he said. "It may not happen in your lifetime or in mine, but it will happen. India will be destroyed and a new nation will arise." What of the suffering, the deaths, the tremendous tragedies, I asked. "The millions who will die in the revolution are nothing compared to the hundreds of millions who die under the colonialism of the capitalistic powers," he replied.

Postscript

T hus we have seen something of the life of Karl Marx in its struggles, crudities, frustrations and successes, with the leading elements of his philosophical and political theories.

In writing the previous pages it occurred to me that Marx was first and last an urban man. He was born in a small city, and after that lived in the largest cities of Europe—Berlin, Paris, Brussels, London. He saw the world from the point of view of the city dweller. In all his writings he pays very little attention to the countryside except as a source of labor for industry. To Marx work meant by and large a laborer's hours in some kind of industrial system, the factory, assembly line, mill, or depths of the mines. The farm laborers of the future socialist state were to be workers in an agricultural factory, as indeed Soviet Russia and China, with the collectivization of the farms, have made them. In *The Communist Manifesto* he speaks favorably of "the abolition of the distinction between town and country" by distributing the population, and he favors the "combination of agriculture with manufacturing industries." Marx fitted his theories into life, history, culture, and civilization as experienced by urban people, even though many of them may have recently come from the land; the rhythm of the agricultural seasons was but a prelude to the rhythm of the machine. Since ninety percent of the masses owned no land, and often not much more than clothing and some furniture, and he himself had no interest in real property, he envisioned all people in the future perfect state as being supremely happy owning nothing. He could not understand the peasants' love for their small holdings or the city dwellers' hope for a garden. Desire for land was a bourgeois characteristic which had to be eliminated. Aside from a few early essays in which he spoke of the plight of wood cutters and wine growers, he was concerned primarily with the struggle of the industrial worker, the slum dweller pitted in a battle to the death with the capitalist who profited from the surplus-value forced out of the workers. The small artisan, the printer, watchmaker, shoe maker, as well as the seamstress and shopkeeper—the very types of people who formed the League of the Just and the Communist League and led him to write the *Manifesto*—were to be absorbed into a factory system, as indeed they have been in most of today's communist nations. The peasant, small farmer, and the small land holder meant nothing to him (other than the danger of

their allying themselves with the bourgeoisie against the workers) until these rural people were transported to the cities to
become forced members of the proletariat. He considered them
"reactionary" because they fear "their impending transfer into
the proletariat," a move he considered beneficial for society. He
was even more bitter about the true outcasts, the lumpen-
proletariat, whom he called the "dangerous class" and the "social scum, the passively rotting mass thrown off by the lowest
layers of old society" who he believed will have no role in the
revolution but that of "a bribed tool of reactionary intrigue."

Thus he has established the concept of the proletariat as a
Chosen People, a concept which remains today among staunch
Marxists, who have accepted his teachings almost literally as a
body of received truths not to be developed or tampered with.
And only certain people are given the grace of interpretation.
In this concept the Chosen People are divided into leaders and
the masses, the leaders' roles being to preserve the True Faith,
rescue the elect, punish the wicked for the sins they have in-
flicted on others, and to establish the Kingdom of Justice on
earth. This is not a fanciful view, for it was quite early realized
and condemned by some of the more observant Marxists. The
German Communist Rosa Luxemburg, a contemporary of Lenin's, argued that according to the views Lenin expressed, "the
mass of comrades [the proletariat] are denigrated to a mass
incapable of judgment." Their essential virtue was " 'discipline,' that is, passive obedience to duty." Luxemburg stated
that socialism is not merely the seizure of the means of power
and the socialization of the sources of production but the awak-
ening of the proletariat. In the true revolution "the masses will
be the active chorus, and the leaders only the 'speaking parts,'
the interpreters of the wills of the masses." And finally, "Only
the working class, by its own activity, can make the word [of

Marx] flesh," an activity that has so far been denied them in any
Marxist state. Luxemburg was murdered in 1919 in a conflict
between radical Marxists, who wanted an immediate revolution
in Germany, though the workers were unprepared, and socialists, who wanted to contain the communists.

More recently, the controversial and radical psychiatrist, the
late Wilhelm Reich, emphasized the point that the Communist
party in partnership with the trade unions of the Communist
states reflects the authoritarian and totalitarian structures of
the bourgeois societies they have replaced; the proletariat is still
in its traditional place at the bottom. Moreover, leaders and
masses live their psychic lives on different planes. Though the
leaders might be involved with the mass struggle around the
world, their own masses are interested only in their immediate
needs, food, shelter, clothing, their relatives and friends, and
the need for sexual outlets.

In his prophetic vision Marx is just as harsh and dogmatic
as the Zwickau prophets I have mentioned in the Introduction.
He has spoken "scientifically" and to counter him would be
unscientific. No alternatives to his theories are allowed. He is
infallible, as one would expect a religious or spiritual leader to
be. When he shifts position, rejects what he has previously
preached, or compromises with the enemy, it is because his
wisdom is superior, his view is wider. When he makes an ar-
rangement with the enemy, it is for the good of the revolution,
and but for the immediate moment. Others who compromise
are not "historically correct." And in Marxism, either in Marx
himself or his followers, especially those who rule governments
or lead communist parties, there is no such thing as an objective
truth, existing regardless of circumstances and events. Truth is
what serves the needs of the present. Truth, in the eyes of
Marxists, is class-conditioned. Objective truth is a bourgeois

fantasy, to be superseded by historically correct proletarian truth. This has led, and still leads, to a rewriting of the past and of claims for communism that in fact may have no connection with it but are of value for the class struggle. Thus, in Russia, numerous loyal dedicated communists could be shot, exiled, or imprisoned; at best they were written out of existence. The great Leon Trotsky, a brilliant theoretician, strategist, and soldier, and one of the founders of the Soviet, disappeared from Marxist writings of all types because he disagreed with Lenin and Stalin. Trotsky, like many others, became a non-person. In different editions of the Soviet Encyclopedia, people, events, and nations regularly disappear, or reappear, according to their usefulness to the revolution.

The instability of truth, as well as the insistence on the special grace of the Chosen People, has led to a strange paralysis of development in Marxism. The French writer and philosopher, Jean-Paul Sartre, for a time an active communist, noted:

> Marxism, after drawing us to it as the moon draws the tides, after transforming all our ideas, after liquidating the categories of our bourgeois thought, abruptly left us stranded . . . it no longer had anything new to teach us, because it had come to a stop. Marxism stopped. . . . Marxism possesses theoretical bases, it embraces all human activity; but it no longer *knows* anything.

Marx's future world forces a brutal break with the past. And not only with the European past but all pasts and presents, too, for he saw the great civilizations of Asia, Africa, and the Americas only as preliminaries for a Marxist Europeanization. Others' customs, handicrafts, technologies, forms of self-government, ways of life, arts, myths, religions were but curiosities that would vanish in the comradeship of the factory, mine, mill,

and self-eliminating bureaucracy of the socialist state. All had
to be destroyed to be saved. His new world would be neat,
tidy, ordered, disciplined, self-directing, rational, above all,
scientific, processed through his computer-like mind. Much of
this feeling is undoubtedly due in part to his own disordered
life, in part to his real rage at the injustices he saw all about him.
But in the end it was implacable economic law which domi-
nated everything. Nevertheless, millions of men and women
have accepted these coldly scientific plans for their future because they are able to inject their own warm humanity into
them.

In criticism of Marx's implacable science, another great
thinker, Sigmund Freud (born in 1856, while Marx was living
in obscurity in London), stated:

> It cannot be assumed that economic motives are the only ones
> that determine the behaviour of human beings in society. The
> undoubted fact that different individuals, races and nations
> behave differently under the same economic conditions is alone
> enough to show that economic motives are not the sole dominat-
> ing factors. It is altogether incomprehensible how psychological
> factors can be overlooked where what is in question are the
> reactions of living human beings.

Freud could also remark in criticism:

> There are assertions contained in Marx's theory which have
> struck me as strange: such as that the development of forms of
> society is a process of natural history, or that changes in social
> stratification arise from one another in the manner of a dialecti-
> cal process. I am far from sure that I understand these assertions
> aright; nor do they sound to me "materialistic" but, rather, like
> a precipitate of obscure Hegelian philosophy in whose school
> Marx graduated. I do not know how I can shake off my lay

opinion that the class structure of society goes back to the struggles which, from the beginning of history, took place between human hordes only slightly differing from each other. Social distinctions, so I thought, were originally distinctions between clans or races. . . .

Yet in the end we are still struck with the fact that no matter how much and in what manner we criticize Marx and communism, the Marxist-centered nations share the leadership of the world with the so-called capitalistic countries, this within a mere sixty years of history. And the other third, the impoverished Third World, which includes India, Latin America, the Philippines and Indonesia, Black and Muslim Africa, contain powerful communist movements, often illegal but still forces that cannot be overlooked. Even in Europe there is a resurgence of communism.

In all the communist nations, whether Russia, China, central Europe, or southeast Asia, it is true that a minority of Marxists has been able to establish itself over the non-Marxist majority. The Marxists are well organized, often selfless and altruistic and willing to make personal sacrifices the others will not make. The victory of north Vietnam over the south is a simple example of that, for the people of the south had neither the will, the leaders, nor the program to maintain their independence. And as I conclude this book, bitter struggles are taking place in Asia and Africa, with the likelihood that in most cases, if not all, the Marxists, will eventually win. Certainly non-Marxists have no programs to offer other than opposition and generalities, for the fact is that the alternatives lack any coherent plan, method, or theory. Any foreigner who has seen people starving and jobless in an undeveloped country can realize plainly why men and women will favor Marxism, with its promise of a restructuring

of society, jobs, food, housing, and freedom from oppression—
all offered by Marxists who are also fellow nationals—in preference to intangibles voiced by industrialists, landowners, or even
foreign companies. The Marxist can, and does, say: throw out
the capitalists who are exploiting you, throw out the colonialists
who take our wealth from us, and we will give everyone a job.
The capitalist can make no such promises, for then he will no
longer be a capitalist.

Moreover, much as the established communist countries
show a grave tendency to wobble and crack under the pressures
of their own inefficiencies and poor leadership, capitalism today, as Marx predicted, is facing its own dilemmas. The free
world is experiencing a series of crises, running from "rolling
readjustments" to recessions to depressions, and is marked by
continual unemployment, inflation, social chaos, weakening
currencies, and a general devaluation of standards. And
anarchism, that once-possible alternative of Godwin's, Proudhon's, and Bakunin's, which proposed a system of local and
regional autonomous councils, communes, and governments
run by elected representatives, was in the past so harmed by the
violence of certain of its members that now few people will
consider it as a possible alternative. Socialism of the nonviolent
type has evolved into such a powerful central state in countries
like Sweden that the rights of the individual are often threatened, with no resulting benefit for society as a whole.

Today, no matter how much of Marx we might accept or
reject, he is still with us to the end, forcing us to question our
institutions, our society, our forms of government, our very way
of life. Marx is with us like the Spectre of the *Manifesto* as we
debate how far we should extend out welfare programs, how
much aid —"welfare capitalism"—is to be given to big business, what to do about strikes and layoffs, raw materials, mar-

kets, planned obsolescence, ecology. Whoever, whatever, we are, Marx is a living, angry power in our lives, forcing us to examine as in a mirror, what he so aptly termed our "naked self-interest."

Index